Inspirations

From

GOD

Vol. 1

D.S. Dennis

ISBN 978-1-64114-776-7 (paperback)
ISBN 978-1-64114-777-4 (digital)

Christian Faith Publishing, Inc.
832 Park Avenue
Meadville, PA 16335
www.christianfaithpublishing.com

Printed in the United States of America

This entire work is inspired by God,
but the words spoken by God are in quotation marks.

Introduction

The different aspects of Christ, from the birth to the resurrection, each in themselves tell a story. A deep need for mankind to know and understand all there is about these happenings of Christ has been with us from the beginning.

Praise God for the prophets of old who wisely recorded each avenue of thought given by God.

Hail to the disciples who gave an accurate account, each in and of themselves, of the life of Christ and their experiences with him. Halleluiah to a glorious King, and praise his name forever and ever.

A Tribute

Dear, Lord Jesus, guide me this day
while I'm at work and at play.

There couldn't be a better guide
if I were to search this planet far and wide.

The many lives you've led your way,
I could not begin to know how many each day.

Groping through the dark must be a lonely life;
why can't they all turn to you and begin a new life?

Each day they wait, you might say, "Sorry, it's too late";
oh, how can I tell them not to wait?

When I see small children being led astray,
I pray, Lord Jesus, that soon you'll take over and lead the way.

So many lives are lost due to war, it's true;
but why little children, I know now they're with you.

But it hurts, Lord Jesus, to see how war hurts us so,
and I pray someday soon you'll come to stay and not go.

There will be change when you're in charge;
I'll praise God the Father for putting you in charge.

Oh, worship the King, oh, my soul, this I plead;
praise God the Father, Son, and Holy Ghost, these I'll heed.

A Haven

Lord Jesus, my Redeemer and Savior to be,
my Refuge, my Haven, please give it to me.

Let your light shine through my entire life,
a beacon to those in misery and strife.

May I always be humble, honest, and caring
to those with heartaches, your love always sharing.

Not wanting to be all calloused and hollow,
wherever you lead me, Lord, may I follow.

Glory Be to God on High

Hosea

Glory be to God on high, whatever be thy will;
I come before you, God, to pray whate'er it be, your will instill.

Upon my heart, I heed the cry of love to share
with all your children, a responsibility we bear.

Come, O Lord, come be my guide to eternal life;
this is our need, not our strife.

What burdens we bear are only to prepare us
so what lies ahead might not scare us.

Praise him, praise him, praise him, God in heaven on high;
all the saints adore him, our God to us draw nigh.

If it is our Father's will,
we the people will instill.

Our hearts and minds are full of love
for our Father up above.

Cling to all he says to you,
for you can believe it's true.

Hearts directed up above
will always be filled with his love.

"Don't discourage when I withhold my touch;
be patient, you expect too much.

9

In good time, I will reveal
to you and all how I feel.

With hope and faith you have in your heart,
believe me when I say I'll never depart.

Prepare yourself for service to me, and believe I am one in three,
better known as the Trinity."

My Prayer
St. John 19

O Jesus, how we love you, for you died to save us,
doing only your Father's will, for each sin He forgave us.

Keeping only unto him,
you saved us all from our sin.

I pray you will forgive me now
when I find it difficult to bow.

Humble me if I might ask,
so I can proceed with your task.

To do your work is my whole life;
hold me close during strife.

Just as you provide strength for all,
strengthen me after my fall.

Build on me, your servant to be;
I do believe all things are possible with thee.

I cannot wish it and it be so;
I must wait patiently, I know.

O, the reverence I feel;
please everything, be still.

Working for God

O Lord God, our heavenly Father, come be our guide,
if we can only withstand the test of time without ever a slide.

We'll be servants of yours with only one goal:
to witness to those who have lost their soul.

Whate'er be the message, Lord, you can depend on us
to do whate'er we must.

Wagging Tongues

O Lord Jesus, be thou our guest.
If we should gossip or talk out of line,
please see that we recognize our misdeed,
for if we should lose you, oh, how we'd pine.

The Problem
Romans 8:31–39
2 Corinthians 6:1–10

O Lord God, what is it I'm to do;
should I go and tell them all just what I've been up to?

Should I let it all pour out, or does it have to be;
whatever it is, Lord, with you I must agree.

I praise you for this problem, for through it, I will grow;
to be a better Christian is the direction I must go.

Are you trying to tell me not today?
Are you trying to tell me think and pray?

What if this is a moment lost?
"Be patient, child, count the cost."

If only I knew for sure what you want me to say,
or is it just that you want me to forget it and pray?

What is it, Lord, you would have me to do?
Is it best to think this problem through before coming to you?

If I search the scriptures through and through,
will I find my answer? Will it be of you?

You've helped me before in finding my way;
I know you'll guide me day by day.

All I need is faith and an open ear,
then trust it is you that I'll hear.

Leading me onward and upward to stay,
closer and closer with praise do I pray.

So if it is your will, Lord, then into it I must plunge;
it seems to me right now, Lord, to be the final plunge.

But through it all, I know, Lord, you'll hold me close to you;
that beacon of light from heaven above will be your love, that
will see me through.

Talking and Listening to God

"Keep going, I mean to say.
It isn't what is to happen today."

"You see, child, you jumped too fast.
You didn't stop to listen after you ask."

Did I misunderstand the whole ordeal?
"You know you didn't stop to think how I feel."

What if I were to lose you now?
"You will never lose me, child, not now."

"Not for such a small error as this.
It's just part of your training gone amiss."

"Tell me now, haven't I reassured you?
To know I have control over you."

"Give up this fretting and trying so hard to find your way.
Relax with me, I'll guide you forever along my way."

"Tomorrow will always be beautiful, you'll see.
For I'll open your eyes to many secrets of me."

"Keeping your eyes upon me is important, you know.
For then as I have your attention, the blessings will flow."

"Give up fretting and worrying so.
I know you love me."

"I know you love me, so don't despair
when you think that I think that you don't care."

16

"I'll always be guiding you step by step,
watching and laughing and loving each step."

"Knowing you'll always be looking to me
for that guidance and laughing and loving to see."

"Keep your head held high, and don't look down,
for you'll be part of my kingdom, you'll receive your crown."

"Always keep an ear open for what I might say.
It just might be I'll need your help today."

"In finding lost souls and filling them full
will be your glory but not always the rule."

"There'll be other tasks I'll ask you to do.
I'm sure you'll be able, if only you knew."

So keep your eyes on Jesus today.
"And always remember I'm with you to stay."

O Lord God, how I love thee;
to think you really care so much about me.

Thank You, Lord

Oh, thank you, Lord, for each new day,
for all creation, and being able to pray.

Thank you, Lord, for apples in the fall,
for flowers in the spring, and James, John, Peter, and Paul.

Thank you, Lord, for all our trees,
for with pollution today, they help us breathe.

Thank you, Lord, for garter snakes and bullfrogs,
for all the work they do for us, just think of the hours they've
logged.

Thank you, Lord Jesus, for being my friend.
For in time of need, you always have a helping hand to lend.

Thank you, Lord, for a husband that's ill,
for I'll appreciate him and the idle hours we have to fill.

Thank you, Lord, for sisters, brothers, fathers, and mothers,
for family of any size is very important, not just these but, too,
all the others.

So thank you, Lord, for each new day,
for all the time we have on earth to stay.

Thank you, Lord, for winter, spring, summer, and fall,
for each has its purpose and, oh, the beauty of it all.

Thank you, Lord, for being able to say
thank you for this new day.

Thank you, Lord, for every minute I've been saved,
for we never know how much time we've wasted till we've
given in to the Lord and prayed.

All of this the Lord has made me aware of;
if you'll give in, you'll always be taken care of.

No more fretting or stewing or fuming to get you down;
just pleasure, peace of mind, deeper love, and rest assured,
with all forgiven, in your sins you'll not drown.

Forge Ahead

O Lord Jesus, come be my guest;
through the space of time, let me pass the test.

Watch over all my family, Lord, keep them near and dear;
hold them close, Lord, so they will not fear.

Hope is for the future, we're not to worry what is past;
give to my family, Lord, a life that will last.

For the Group

O Father in heaven, please hear our plea;
come be our guide, O how we worship thee.

Praises to sing will be our goal;
O Lord, we praise you for the blessings that flow.

Keep us close to you so we might know
just what we're to do; this will help us grow.

If all this is for nothing, Lord,
then we certainly will be of one accord.

But we know with you, Lord,
everything is the truth, Lord.

We'll continue to seek and continue to find;
this you have promised, this we'll keep in our minds.

Opening doors is your job we know,
we'll keep knocking, Lord, for this is how we grow.

Keep opening those doors, Lord, and help us to find
that beautiful friendship that gives peace of mind.

I Feel His Touch

I feel his touch whene'er dark shadows grow;
I feel his touch, and I want the world to know.

I feel his touch when I'm upset,
when mad at the kids, or upset with a pet.

I feel his touch when there's not enough time,
and I yell at the kids, "Come on, we'll be late one more time."

I feel his touch when I've said something I shouldn't
and hurt someone's feelings and to say I'm sorry, I couldn't.

I feel his touch when I've been a gossip,
then gossiping right on, just could not stop it.

I feel his touch at the close of the day,
when peace fills my heart and I remember he's there to stay.

No matter what I've done throughout the day,
just asking forgiveness is what I must pray.

He'll help each one of us very much;
just keep yourself open, and you'll feel that touch.

Yes, Lord, with each hour I feel that love,
whether in guilt from my misdeed or joy from seeing a dove.

I can't say no to his touch;
I love him too much.

Some Day Soon

"Someday soon, when leaves begin to fall,
you be ready to heed my call.

I'll call you to service when the time is right;
just be prepared to fight the fight, to turn wrong to right.

Someday soon, you be ready now;
I can't tell you how important is readiness to bow.

I'll prepare you with knowledge and wisdom,
but you must be willing to leave without feeling imprisoned.

You are free to do just as you choose,
but from what you tell me, you'll be willing to lose.

Just keep your head high, and you must not worry, you know;
everything will be settled and taken care of, you'll be able to go.

Someday soon, just think what a service you'll be;
pray for it to come, for you'll be serving me.

Just think you'll have an answer to a prayer;
yes, I heard you asking to be useful, so prepare.

Just remember to lean on me when you have a load to bear;
I'll be there, I really do care."

When Duty Calls

Is there something I'm to do, Lord?
Could it be you're trying to tell me, Lord?

If only my head weren't so thick, Lord;
I could think of it just real quick, Lord.

O Lord, what a beautiful countryside;
makes one want to run and hide.

Away from all the business of the day,
away from the hustle and bustle to stay.

But we can't do that and still serve thee, Lord,
for it's people with whom we're concerned, Lord.

I pray that I'll serve you the best I know how, Lord,
knowing you'll guide me every step of the way, Lord.

I pray that someday soon you'll tell me what I'm to be;
I pray that knowledge and wisdom is sufficient when asked to
follow thee.

Every time I stop to pray, I get the feeling there should be more
to me;
I know someday you'll reveal this to me, and it will be of thee.

Soon I'll know my specific task,
then I pray you'll fill me with wisdom and knowledge, this I ask.

Only then can I do a decent job for you, Lord;
this power and strength, wisdom and knowledge must come
from you, Lord.

Thank you, Lord, for what I am;
I pray you'll make of me whate'er you can.

Opening New Doors

If there's a certain prayer that should be prayed,
then Father, please help me to pray it;
if there's someone who needs encouragement,
then Father, please help me to say it.

Hoping beyond hope that your Spirit will lead me,
then confident that if asked, he surely will;
praying for guidance is important for us all,
for without it, we our own thoughts might instill.

This would mean failure, for how could we know
just what's in the heart of those whom we're leading;
surely the Spirit would keep us from hurting,
but Satan's in there, guiding astray with a power unyielding.

So be sure when we're guiding a person's soul,
we have the Holy Spirit within us to form each word;
then pray to be open for the Spirit to guide us,
then sit back and watch the Lord do his work undisturbed.

We must be one with the Lord, one with the Spirit;
we must be full and open to be useful to him.
So pray to your Father and ask for that filling,
then praise him and thank him for your deliverance from sin.

Opening new doors to new hearts is our goal,
always asking for guidance along the way;
serving our Lord by spreading his message,
growing to know our Savior day by day. He is our friend to stay.

Gossip
James 3

Love thy neighbor as thyself is very profound indeed;
it's difficult, Lord, but I can see the need.

I'm as guilty as can be, Lord, with my gossiping;
I've caused my Spirit to grieve, and I need forgiving.

But I can't forgive myself of the damage I might have done;
I pray I can undo it, for my agony is wondering if she heard it.

I pray I didn't hurt her and she knows not what was said;
in time we can, with your help, make amends.

To do that, I must change my own heart;
I must not keep grieving the Spirit and driving him apart.

I plead with you, Lord, to help me to find that unselfish love,
then once conquered, Lord, again I'll see the dove.

Let Thy Will Be Mine

O heavenly Father, how precious thy name,
your cross to bear when we were to blame.

How deep was your love;
how much we needed the dove.

How gracious your mercy
when we were not worthy.

If only our love could be as thine,
then as a witness, we'd surely shine.

Continue to fill us so thy sheep we might feed;
this be our glory, our witness, our deed.

Thank you, O Father, most precious and divine,
that our will is thy will. Yes! Let it be thine.

The Trinity

The Trinity, the three in one, is all we think and much more still. Whenever we say our call to worship, we need to remember just whom we are addressing.

What we all need is an understanding of our Savior's greatness. This will give us some idea of the overall vastness of the Trinity.

"Don't think I'm trying to upset you with this profound statement. I only want to impress on your minds just what you're dealing with. Don't think for a moment that any of what I tell you is not of me.

The entire scope of the Trinity you cannot understand, but you all need to open your hearts and minds to let a full measure of your comprehension expound on the greatness therein.

Praise your God the Father, Son, and Holy Ghost, for there is more to this ritual than you understand.

Try to retain your insight into the meaning of your church liturgy. Open your mind to praise, and pray for understanding. This is your way of comprehending my greatness.

Pray without ceasing. Understanding will come in time. Keep your eyes on his greatness, and praise will flow from your minds. Then joy will fill your hearts as you've never known. Think now! Isn't it when you praise him that the love fills and overflows the heart? Making joy uncontrollable. Give all of yourselves to praising him; call on him for anything. When he knows how you've praised his greatness, he'll respond before you expect it."

The Lord, your God, is just waiting to pour out upon you the gifts of the Spirit. But first, your praise and understanding of the greatness therein must flow from your heart.

Praise him, praise him, praise him, all the saints adore him. Glory be to his name.

Remain Close

O Lord God, what's wrong with me that I can't hear you too well;
I know that it's me. I've shut a door, and I've slipped and fell.

I never want to lose what you've given me;
somehow you must point to my error and save me.

This continual nagging that I've pushed you away,
it just can't be, for I very much need you to stay.

So I praise you, Lord, for your greatness today
and pray you'll impart some wisdom my way.

Then just maybe I'll be smart enough next time to know when
I'm going wrong
and turn it around before I do too much damage and become
so forlorn.

So fill me again, Lord, let my cup overflow;
light that torch within so once more I might glow.

For it's your glory we must proclaim,
and without your fire, I'm like a horse gone lame.

Can't do much good that way, and horses they shoot;
if I'm to be your witness, I've got to show I give a hoot.

I'm just too bogged down with duties, I know.
If it's your wish, give me strength so I can do them and grow.

As it stands now, my mind's all aclutter;
I get so nervous, my heart's all aflutter.

Calm me and comfort me, Lord, I do pray;
teach me, when approached for duties, just what I should say.

I praise you, dear Lord, for the knowledge you impart,
and thank you for this poem, Lord, for now I've got my start.

Battling Satan

O heavenly Father, what is your charge?
Will we respond? Will the task be too large?

Day after day, we listen for your call,
hoping upon hope that we're not too small.

Understanding is necessary, yet first, we must hear;
whate'er the message, we must not fear.

Fear is the beginning of a feeling of inadequacy;
it comes from Satan, he has a lot of audacity.

All the feelings we dislike in ourselves come from the pit;
this is why we must lean on Jesus to keep us from becoming sick.

Sick of ourselves, sick of our brothers, nothing can suit;
this is Satan's glory when we become destitute.

Satan will help us drive and beat down the Spirit within us,
for when we have done so, Jesus just doesn't seem near us.

So when these feelings overwhelm us once more,
just say, "Satan, leave me in the name of Jesus Christ," then
shut the door.

Now you'll have to be ready, for Satan will try again;
through fear, hatred, gossip, anxiety, these are of him.

But we know, don't we, with Jesus in our hearts,
that we can conquer these feelings and have a fresh start.

Just turn your eyes to heaven, battle evil thoughts with good,
plead with Jesus to help us, and you'll be understood.

Ask him to refill you when you've beaten down the Spirit;
tell him that you're sorry, and he will commandeer it.

Then keep your eyes on Jesus, and remember what you've been
through;
the next time you start slipping, you'll remember, and you'll
stay true.

True to Jesus Christ, true to the Spirit within;
then it will be easy to turn away from sin.

Keep that loyal heart, keep it till the end;
then you'll hear what Jesus tells you, you'll hear and understand.

Open the Door

Father, Lord Jesus, my Savior supreme,
what is your message for us this day?
Will it be a lesson we must learn for ourselves?
Or will you guide us in your special way?

"Yes, my children, you'll learn of me today.
You'll learn, and I'll guide you each step of the way.
For all your life you have needed a hand
to lead you and guide you so you would understand.

I'll keep this promise I made with you,
and you'll understand eventually what I have planned;
just keep yourself open so I can come in and work through
you.
This is what you must do to receive my guidance and
understand.

Keep a sensitive ear and a sensitive heart,
be always alert to recognize it's me;
help those around you understand me also.
Reassure them this message is not of thee but of me.

Keep your mind open to receive me always.
I'll not disappoint you by remaining far off;
I'm always waiting for you to open the door.
This is the only way I'll enter your life."

Walking Close with the Lord

Walking close with the Lord should be a daily experience,
one that is refreshing and enjoyable.
If you're walking there, it will surely be evident,
and if you're not, your life may seem deplorable.

Believe it or not, the Lord is always there,
whether you recognize his presence is quite another thing;
he'll never leave you once you've said you're his,
and he is what gives life the reason for being.

So hold your head high, but don't become proud.
Give him the lead at the start of the day;
if you've asked that he lead you in each encounter,
he'll lead you and guide you. He'll show you the way.

The life you live with Jesus at the helm
will be a life worth more than treasures of gold;
so ask him in to mold your will,
then start your walk with that Redeemer of old.

Our Prayers

We want what we want so much of the time;
we don't stop to consider the reason or rhyme.

We just keep asking for all that we're worth,
expecting to gain for ourselves more power on earth.

"Just stop to think that without me, you would not be.
When you pray for more power, there is also more responsibility to me.

I love you and will give you only what you can handle,
so keep asking for guidance in handling that which I've given.

Don't ask for so much that you become overwhelmed;
ask that instead of you trying to manage it, I be at the helm.

Consider your motives in pleading your cause;
be sure that you're honest without e'er a flaw.

Don't delve too quickly into works you think are of me;
stop to consider my wishes, then let it at my guidance be.

Quick actions can sometimes do harm and bring you grief;
wait for my guidance in all things, this must be your belief.

Pray for my presence in all situations,
then you can depend that you'll have the best answer for all
altercations.

Always pray without ceasing, talk to me always.
Our communication will grow, and you'll do your best always.

So keep that channel open at all times of the day,
and don't forget to rely on me and pray, pray, pray.

It's when you let your mind stray to the worry of your world
that you get in trouble and problems are unfurled.

So keep your eyes on Jesus, just what would he want you to do;
this is the basis for successful living for you."

Linda and David Look Up

"This is the beginning of a new life for both of you.
Cherish it contentedly, hold close to the idea you are one;
never let the darkness of sorrow give you doubts of me.
Cling forever to the idea that within me lies your salvation.

The road may be stony and hard when first traveled upon,
so many new things to learn of each other,
but when eyes are turned upon me, your Savior,
self is forgotten; your aim will be to please each other.

Come unto your Christ with all your problems.
Never try to solve them without me.
The small as well as the overpowering ones,
when laid at my feet, will fade away from thee.

As you travel through life together, continually relying on me,
you'll find that stony road will turn into a path of sand
as each of you become respectively closer, and yes, as one,
your union with each other and together with me will be grand

Open your eyes to the sin around you, and pray for these, my children.
Open your hearts as well;
serve me well with your prayers and witness.
Continually contact through prayers and deeds, you must dwell.

Consider your life with me as one great chord of a song,
with each aspect of your lives well blended with me;
be assured that each of you will see me someday
because of the Lord Jesus. This is the promise of the Trinity."

Assurance

O Lord Jesus, come dwell within.
Help drive away that wicked old sin.

O Lord Jesus, what can I say
but ask that you lead me each day
.

Whate'er may happen to fill me with fear,
I call on your name, and it will soon disappear.

I know you'll be there whene'er I call,
waiting to lift me from each little fall.

Oh yes! I'll slip as most humans do,
but I know that I have you to see me through.

"Oh yes! My child, you have me to lean on.
And when need be, I'll be there with bells on.

Remember to always look up to me,
to listen and hear what I expect of thee.

Never doubt that, when you call, I will come,
for I'll never let you fall to where you came from.

Hold tight to your Lord Jesus with all your might;
don't say it's too difficult and give up the fight.

Sure, Satan will tear at you most of the time
until you're beyond your testing and reach the sublime.

I'll hold you close, just cling to me;
don't let go of what you have, I ask this of thee.

Take up your cross and bear it; be bold,
just as I did for you in days of old.

Your life right now, I know, isn't easy;
remember what you're working for doesn't come easy.

I love you, my child, and this you can depend on;
have you forgotten what I've done for you already.

Gird up your spirits and praise me once more;
continue to have faith and the blessings will flow.

A heart always full of sadness just can't be,
for I love you and you must remember to turn to me.

Hold on, the battle isn't over yet,
for you need pruning but with love you can bet.

And when you become that person I want,
believe me, you'll be chosen to sit at my table, right up front."

Is There Something Stirring You?

O Lord God Almighty, how wonderful thy name;
do we really realize the greatness of that refrain?

Is there something stirring you and you wonder what it is?
Could it be the touch of God calling you to be his?

Do you find your life distraught, problems everywhere abounding?
If you turn it over to the Lord, the peace you'll feel is simply astounding.

Can you let the Lord guide your life? That means lead you day by day?
If you can let it be, your life will blossom, and you'll be so much happier doing it his way.

Busy Works

O heavenly Father, Lord God from above,
please let us always sing praises with love.

"To keep up with busy works is not what I want of you.
So put them aside, and be still long enough to hear what you're
to do.

This matter of running to and fro, to please oneself, on impulse,
is not of my calling and displeases me; I'm at a loss.

For while you're busy flitting about, you can't hear or feel me,
you're not doing my will;
so rise each morning with this question to me, what is your
calling for this new day, Lord? Your will I want to fulfill.

I guide you each day but keep in contact throughout;
your days will be filled with many new adventures, and you'll
be at peace without a doubt.

This close contact is important as we walk through your life;
you'll find a friend in me, your guiding light, in sorrow and
strife.

I'll never give you a task you're unable to handle,
for in our close walk, I'll give you the path to follow.

Remember always to turn to me in everything you do;
let me plan your days, they'll be better by far and keep that ear
in tune. That's what I ask of you."

If This Is Life, Who Needs It?

This message was meant for a special person I hardly knew but apparently was very important to the Lord, as are all persons. The beatitudes were to play a very important part along with this poem. Matthew's fifth chapter held the key.

"So many times, we see only beyond our noses and fancy ourselves well versed;
this I don't understand at all when it's I that should be put first.

If only you would see your need to open your heart to me;
don't hold back what needs so desperately to come out, give it all up to me.

Let all the problems of life be shared by me;
this is necessary if I'm to move any closer to thee.

Don't keep putting me off, when in reality, you need me so desperately;
I have so many blessings to give you for your own prosperity.

You must keep your eyes on me and give up the self;
this is a must before I can work through your life or even be of help.

Remember I love you dearly and don't intend to lose you;
so put aside trifles and call on my name to see you through.

Don't look back to worldly idols after you've put them aside,
for your salvation, from now on, only I can be your guide."

Sincerely from
Your loving Redeemer

Why Is It?

"Why is it with the children you always fight?
Do you think you really have a right?

Stop! Return to your childhood;
now do you remember? Your mother never understood.

Could you bring yourself to rise above the squabble,
maybe even talk as if you might like them a little?

It's difficult when you see yourself only as trainer;
can you please see the whole picture? Give me the reins."

Despair

O Father, come be my guest;
Father, please give me rest.

"Seek to find all necessary angles to faith.
Keep in mind your main objective in your faith.

There are many ways in which to keep a close relationship with me.
I will continually draw you into that closer relationship with me.

When you give of yourself totally, then you will find peace.
As of now, you haven't been able to do this with ease.

Someday you'll find what you're looking for,
but only if you continue to seek will I open a new door.

Relax in your prayers, let the truth flow,
then the answers will come, and you'll start to grow.

This growth will take time and much searching on your part,
but if you keep your eyes on me, then it will grow easier with each new start.

Patience and faith will be necessary, look how far you've come.
You've still much to accomplish in learning of me, just think where it's coming from.

I'll continue to guide you and lead you down each new path,
holding you close as you choose each step on that path.

You may stumble a bit or even fall and bruise a knee.
Just get right back up, and remember to keep your eyes upon me.

Then only as you see the light of your problem will you become in tune with me.
Growing much closer and feeling the love and warmth I'm waiting to pour out upon thee."

Strength from the Spirit

O heavenly Father, come be my guest;
give me on paper just what I should attest.

"O child of mine, I give you love,
so let it shine like the Son above.

O child of mine, you've got to speak.
My Spirit, through you, will strengthen the weak.

O child of mine, give to me the control.
Through words that I give, teach how to extoll."

O Father above, how can I lead?
"Only with my strength can you succeed.

Remember to call on me in your time of need.
I'll be there to take the lead.

Now keep in mind, you go with love.
In heaven above, you'll see the dove."

An Important Message

This was an important message for a rebellious young man whom I had never met, but through compassion given by the Lord, I was made aware of his family's concern.

O heavenly Father, what is it today?
Is it that I'm just to pray?

What is it, Father, I'm to say?
Is this poem maybe for Ray?

"Come, let me tell you what this is about.
Just understand why this must come out.

We have a problem, both you and I.
This much I can tell you, listen or die.

You may not have another chance with me,
so forget right now what's so important to thee.

I can't help you or give you peace
until you come to me and let it all release.

This much you know, you've been brought up well,
so what's so difficult? Why must you be a hard sell?

Open your heart, and listen to me.
This will be of help to you if you'll only let it be.

Now open your mind, and think of me.
Let those close to you tell you of me.

Listen and accept it, it's very real, you know.
You need this, or I wouldn't be telling you so.

So fall to your knees, and let pride go out the door.
I'll give you much more, something really worth living for.

I'll give you peace in that scrambled mind,
if you'll just give in and let me give to you the sublime.

Material wealth will never give you peace.
That human need for more just never will cease.

Your friends of the street can't give you eternal life.
They can only give misery and strife.

So take it from me, your loving Father above,
you need Jesus, you need love."

Trees

Dear God in heaven, how beautiful are your trees;
so lovely and wonderful are all these.

With arms outstretched, reaching toward the sky,
as if praising their Father and Creator on high.

If these trees could talk, what stories they could tell,
watching each generation cast its spell.

Seeing each family grow and mature,
when growing with God, they're safe and secure.

We see much of God's wisdom in these beautiful trees;
just stop and think what they give, if you please.

They provide for many of our life-giving needs;
let's see if we can think of some of these.

Let's start with the air, they provide oxygen, you know;
then there's moisture they hold in the earth so things grow.

They help break up strong currents of wind as they blow;
this prevents erosion of soil as you know.

We could go on for quite a while,
for trees fit into each one's lifestyle.

So let us thank God for this beautiful gift;
just to look at their beauty provides a lift.

We should take a lesson from these trees,
always giving of ourselves for others, if you please.

Childlike Faith
Hebrews 11:1-13 / Romans 5:1-5

Childlike faith, just what do they mean?
Let's examine what this could be.

Could it mean the faith of a little girl in her father
as she looks at her broken doll and says,
"It will be all right, Mommy. Daddy will fix it."

Oh, for such faith in my Father above,
trusting he'll fix my everyday problems through his love.

Could it mean the faith of a little boy in his father
as he thinks to himself, *If I tell Dad I'm sorry, but it was
really me who broke that window, I know he'll forgive me.*

Thank you, Father, for sending Jesus our Savior to be,
for all my sins, I can say, "Father, forgive me."

Childlike faith, what a joy it can be
to be able to know for certain that I have life eternally.

Let's Give Thanks
1 Timothy 4:14–16

O heavenly Father, thank you for this new day,
for the sunshine and the children at play.

Thank you for the hearts you've touched
by working through us this much.

Thank you, Lord, for the sharing we can do;
this is necessary in helping us understand you.

This much I know, we all need continual contact with you;
otherwise, we'd fail in our work that you give us to do.

Just think how we'd thirst if you didn't fill our cup,
yet all we have to do is ask, and you'll fill it up.

And we ask, Lord, that you fill it with love and compassion,
so we can be of help to those troubled after a fashion.

But first we must pray for guidance from above,
for without it, we'd cause more turmoil through our love.

So let's keep our eyes on Jesus throughout our witness for the Lord;
it will be exciting, I guarantee you'll not be bored.

For Karen P.
Matthew 5:1-20

"The only way you can go is forward now;
this will bring us together in the future, you'll see how.

I only want what is best for you at this point of your life,
even though you must go through some misery and strife.

Hang on to my word, you know it's from me;
repeat them over, and Satan will flee.

You have nothing to fear for you're in my hands,
and I'll see you through all problems of these lands.

Hold your head high, and depend on me fully
when you feel set apart and tongues become unruly.

Don't resent them, for they don't understand;
forgive them, love them, lend them a hand.

Thirst after righteousness, and continue to be filled;
in this, never cease, and heaven will be revealed.

Grab hold of yourself, for I'm with you always;
take comfort, my child, blessed be thee always."

Living His Way

O heavenly Father, is this the way
we should act on the Lord's day?

"What is the purpose of giving you rest
if you don't take it as being what is best?

Give up your frantic search for food.
You know I'll take care, I thought it was understood.

Whatever the need, I will provide.
All you have to do is recognize and decide.

Decide you need my help and ask for it, that's all.
This is all it takes, for I respond when my children call.

Just keep in touch, and let me have my way.
This is what will provide you an extra good day.

Listen to hear what I want to say to you.
Keep in mind it will be what's best for you too.

Don't put aside the important things of life.
Life won't be worth much if these you sacrifice.

Cling to what's good, make it work for you,
then open your heart, and let my light shine through."

For the Group

This, I felt, was received to be shared with my own prayer and share group.

"Dear children, you've struck upon an important aspect. The questions that fill your minds are important only as a part of learning. You can't possibly find suitable, unquestionable answers to problems that have troubled the universe since the beginning of the gospel. Your faith and trust are the answers to your never-ending questions, and in this, you are growing with each answered prayer. Let your faith and trust be a sufficient guide in daily living. Along with my treasured Word, you couldn't have a better combination. Picking parts out of the Bible and then finding conflicting views in it also can cause turmoil if dwelled upon. Relying on me as a guide when unsure where and how to apply what you've read is the best way to handle it. You were not meant to know all there is to know about any situation. If this were so, you would not need me. Work to grow in faith and trust. Continually pray and ask my guidance. There can be no greater praise to me than my children calling on my name for guidance. Here lies my pleasure, answering the prayers of my children and strengthening their faith and trust. Awaken your minds, be alert, it pleases me to see my children joyfully doing my will, with the trust of a little child that all will turn out well. So don't take to heart all the unanswered problems that concern you. Just turn them over and ask for my help. Surely your faith is strong enough to know it can be placed in no better hands. Continue to pray and seek. You are doing well. Just remember I can handle what you cannot."

Your New Life
For Twila S.

"Plan your days and follow them through until you gain control;
see that your work is metered out to best fit your role.

Everything you do can be part of my plan;
seek to fill your day to be as useful as you can.

See that your time with me is set aside;
it's important if I'm to be your daily guide.

I can see you through any and all kinds of problems;
this you know, so take a strong hand in dealing with your
problems.

Pray for my guidance each day from the start,
and you can be sure, in each phase I'll take a part.

I'll lead you if you listen and help you through each day,
and you'll see each day unfolding as you begin to pray.

Don't let the days be wasted, let me help you plan;
you'll find new joy and excitement with each emerging plan.

And as we work together, your life will blossom out;
you'll find true contentment, I'm sure, without a doubt.

So let your love move the mountains out of your way;
rely on me, I'm your guide, here to stay.

Praise me, and you'll find the heavens will open up;
continue to ask for my help, and I will fill your cup.

Don't worry about tomorrow, for I have it planned;
just remember to ask for my guidance, I'll tell you where you
stand.

You are in my care now, so never fret or stew;
you'll always have my love, for this, you can be sure 'tis true."

Waiting on God

Oh, Lord, what is it you want me to do?
Wait it out, is this the rule?

Could it be that I'm not to work?
This was maybe only Satan beginning to lurk.

How could this be explained to Don, as he won't understand?
This could only cause a rift, so it must not be your plan.

You wouldn't want me to hurt, this I do know;
so maybe I should ask you to make my cold go.

So this I am doing, Father, take it from me;
let head and body, from sickness, be free.

Send Satan on his way, Lord, as he has no place in my soul;
I want only Jesus in my heart to make me whole.

And him and I together can do the Lord's work, this I can be
sure;
for with Jesus in my heart, I can resist Satan's lure.

So yes, Jesus, I ask that you guide me each day,
and there in my heart, I want you to stay.

Keep Your Eyes on Jesus

"If there is a need, I shall supply it.
If it takes the form of a job, don't deny it.

Keep your faith and trust in me.
I'll see you'll have my promises, trust me.

Always show gratitude in what you may receive.
Use it wisely to better your life, don't grieve.

Keep your spirits high, I have not pulled away.
Only you can cause a rift, I'm here to stay.

Give me the chance to guide your days.
They will be much better in many ways.

Keep your eyes on Jesus in stormy weather.
I hold and keep you safe, no one could do it better.

Don't let fears overwhelm you where I stand.
You know I'll never take away, this you must understand.

So remember always to set aside each day
a time for us to visit, a time for you to pray.

Whatever direction your earthly life will take,
I'll be there guiding if you'll let me, that's no mistake.

Keep lifting your feet and putting them down.
We'll walk this road together, so wipe away the frown.

There is no time for your worry, so put it aside.
Keep your mind on your Redeemer, in him you'll abide."

A Time to Reflect

O heavenly Father, keep my earthly father safe through the night;
hold him and lift him into the light.

Help him to see what a blessing you are;
I want him to ask for Jesus to come into his heart.

I'll never know just where he stands with you,
but I want what's best, so help him realize the truth.

He needs to understand what the Spirit can do;
he needs a closer walk to see him through.

I love him, you know, and it will hurt to see him go,
but you'll be getting a special person, I'm sure you know.

Don't let him lie and be a burden, for this he will not want,
but prepare him, Lord, so he'll be able to accept what you
want.

Let us keep him with us just as long as we can,
as long as he's healthy and happy, you understand.

We don't want him to suffer and live a nonexistent life,
a life in a bed full of misery and strife.

So you do what you want, you know how I feel,
and if there be sorrow just ahead, help me help the others
through their ordeal.

Keeping in Touch

"Sometime in the near future, we'll see each other.
In all we do together as sister and brother.

This I promise, we'll have a compact life.
You'll still be serving humanity in this life.

Keep in touch with me each day.
I'll keep answering your call, I'm here to stay.

This world will need you for some time to come,
so be sure to keep searching so you'll have resources to draw from.

Stop worrying, fretting, and so on.
You know now, don't you? I'm here to rely on.

Your faith in me is stronger each day.
Your faith in yourself must come along way.

Keep yourself open by prayer to me.
This I need if I'm going to work through thee.

Life will keep you busy, yes, I know,
but there is still time for you to work and grow.

I will see to it there is time for our work.
Relax, you don't have to plan, that's my work.

Let me manage your days, I will do it with care.
All you need to do is keep in contact by prayer.

I'll head you down each new path you take.
Just keep asking for guidance so we don't get lost, for my sake.

For I want a close contact so you'll see clearly the plan,
then you'll know where to turn and how to take a stand.

I think you know by now I've been with you each day.
Just keep on asking, I'm here to stay."

He Stands at the Door and Knocks

Thank you, Father, for your help yesterday;
I'm quite pleased my prayers were answered that way.

To turn to you for everything is quite a wonderful task,
especially when we know you always answer when asked.

I try to do as you ask in 2 Corinthians 6:3:
Flee from those things that might make others flee.

I need your help though, Lord, if I'm to stay clean;
daily guidance and a listening ear to keep my life serene.

A life that when observed by those around me
will be good witness for others, to show them how it can be.

It can be a life filled with peace and good will;
if only we'll let ourselves drink from the well, our fill.

Jesus, you know, is that reservoir we drink from;
a wealth of knowledge can be gained if we will just come.

Come to the well, drink in what you can;
there surely is a place for you to fit in his plan.

He'll love you and keep you quite close to him;
if you'll open the door and let him come in.

This must come first, for he'll not come until asked;
once you do this, there is no turning back.

You're launched on a new life, it's special, you'll see;
a new life to live to the fullest, for now you're free.

Free from the bonds of earthly sins we've committed;
eternal life can be yours, for this we all want if we'll just admit it.

The Guiding Light

Is there a guiding light, and what does it mean to me?
I run outside and look up as far as the eye can see.

The sky is full of clouds tonight, and nary a light in sight,
and yet from somewhere, there seems to be coming a light.

A glow, you might say, a warm feeling inside;
maybe a touch from the Father, a reassurance I can't deny.

If only for a moment it was there, I know it was brief;
so now I feel better, Lord, help now my unbelief.

I know in each life there comes that moment to bear
the doubt that the Christ in our hearts just isn't there.

But, Father, if feelings are so important and mean so much,
then maybe the lack of them means we're not keeping in touch.

In each of our lives, there has been a great revelation,
but what of the times we have doubted the relation?

Keeping our hearts and minds on an even keel
may also mean we're not always going to feel.

Feelings are great, but times when we feel empty
how can we doubt your promise? Isn't our faith aplenty?

We know there is a guiding light, and if anyone should deny it,
send him to us, Lord, to be sure we can't deny it.

So if feelings and faith must run hand in hand,
there is a lot of good Christians feeling robbed of their lampstand.

Strength from Above

"The many problems are keeping you apart from me.
Problems that aren't really problems after all.
We'll still have our work together to perform,
so don't keep worrying that without the group, you'll fall.

There's no backing off, now that you know me,
even when you feel it's best for everyone around.
My work will find a way to get done, for I have a plan,
a plan where God's love, on earth, in a few will abound.

You'll be taken care of, as you can see. I've provided work,
and maybe with a dual purpose in mind,
work that will provide an interest as well as worldly needs.
Then there's also my work to be done on the job to keep in mind.

I'm sure you feel insecure in ability at this time,
but don't feel insecure about our relationship.
For if you continue to pray, I'll continue to answer,
and together, we'll work out the formula to overcome it.

I'll give you guidance, you can be sure of that,
and I'll help you over the hurdles of life right now.
We'll accomplish together what's expected of you,
and if you listen closely, we'll win souls, so take a bow.

I know you feel foolish for being so silly and
not putting your faith and trust where it belongs,
but remember, I'm a forgiving Father. Because of
Christ, my Beloved One, you've been reinstated where you belong.

So hang in there, be patient, don't give up too soon,
for we'll be able to accomplish that job as well.
You know my work will get done possibly without your knowing
just what you've done, but if you look back, something will
ring a bell."

Gods Will is Best

O Jesus, O Jesus, come be my friend.
Just live within my heart.
Keep a close watch on this life of mine.
From the straight and narrow never let me depart.

Friends I'm not free to gather with,
I miss my times of sharing;
the tempo of my life has increased,
and I find myself so rushed, I'm afraid I might stop caring.

Help me, Jesus, to organize it all,
to set a pace where there is time for everything;
I need to see those friends around me,
to hear their good news and share their thinking.

But never would I want what I want
if it's not your will for me,
for though I miss sharing with my friends,
my first desire is serving thee.

So enter in, Lord Jesus, my love.
Guide and direct my life for me;
help me to hear your direction for sure,
and you can use my life if it pleases thee.

Changing Directions

The seasons change but not the Father.
Just as the leaves turn from green to red,
you can bet we can rely on the Father as the one
unchanging force in our world; can you be led?

"I will lead you, if you'll follow, down that
special path I've planned.
It isn't hard to follow if you'll let me
take your hand.

You're bound to fall and stumble,
but don't worry, I've still got ahold.
Just turn to me and say you're sorry,
then remember it's just a part of your mold.

Each and every Christian needs to be molded.
This is important if you're to live a Christian life.
For until you're partially molded,
you can't help others through their misery and strife.

This is what you're here for, to witness and to bear
the cross you carry.
But that load won't seem so heavy
if you'll ask for help, and I'll not tarry.

I'll help you with your burdens,
no matter how large or small.
And you, as my new Christian,
will help lift others from their fall.

Together we can do the Father's work.
I'll lift the burdens, and you give witness of his love.
But first you must let me have control,
so your life will have a new direction, and someday you'll see
my dove."

A New Life to Live
For K.N.

"There are times when everything around us seems to be
against us.
This is what you felt, I know,
but don't get discouraged now that you have your new life to live.
Problems arising won't come as such a blow.

You can take my hand and hang on so you won't fall.
This will be a help when the next problem arises.
Just take your place in my Christian world;
your loved one will come to know and like his new wife before
he even surmises.

You've been through a pretty rough time. I know you're afraid
you'll slide back again,
but you must not be afraid;
keep your eyes on Jesus when the going gets rough,
then it won't rain on your parade.

You have a long road ahead of you, a lot of catching up to do.
You need your friends to see you through;
don't be too proud to ask them for help along the way.
As friends, they couldn't be more true.

Your pride we must get rid of, for this is a self-centered sin,
a stigma in the eye;
your eye through which my light can't shine as long as pride
is there,
so you must be as humble as apple pie.

You'll be my witness someday, of this I am sure,
but first there is a lot to learn for you must grow;
I'll help you along the way, all you need to do is ask.
When you come to know me better, you'll realize the blessings
I can bestow.

With this in your heart,
a last minute call,
a place to come to,
a rescue from a fall.

A time for renewal is here for you;
don't lose it, Karen, take my hand.
Remember to keep your eyes up above,
and claim my promises. On these take a stand."

Matthew 28:20, Philippians 4:13, Romans 8:28, James 1:5–6,
Revelation 3:20
John 3:16, John 14:12–14, Matthew 7:7, Jeremiah 33:3,
Psalm 66:8, 18
Psalm 33:18–20, Psalm 32:6, 8, Genesis 40:8, 1 John 1:9

Claim My Promises

"Claim my promises that bring you life.
Don't hesitate to delve deeply into my book.
You'll find them all waiting there to give you peace.
Search until you find, they're all there so just look.

Christians, be aware of what I give to you.
It's given freely without payment of any kind.
Open your hearts and accept your Lord, Jesus Christ.
That alone is the most precious promise you'll find.

Give of yourselves, give your love, you've received it.
Happiness and peace is yours for the taking.
Cancel all the doubts and fears, for they hurt me.
They mean you don't believe the promises I'm making.

Open your hearts and give of yourselves.
You'll find you can be no happier a person.
It just isn't possible to give love and not feel it,
so live your life as a humble, transparent person.

Others will notice, and they will find a true Christian,
a rock with a firm foundation, a true believer,
meek and humble yet steadfast and strong,
a lover of good, not evil, in whom they see their deliverer.

Cancel the heartaches and pain, the doubts and the worries.
They'll pull you apart from your Blessed Redeemer.
Live for the present as if it were your last on earth,
your last chance to spread the love of Christ, your Redeemer.

So keep a firm grip on the promises in my book.
Learn to practice the way I tell you to live.
Pray for and give love to my people everywhere,
and accept what I so willingly want to give."

Some Days Aren't So Good

"There are some days that aren't so good, it's true.
There are even days that you'll feel quite blue.

It isn't the end of the world to lose a friend, you know.
It's part of a plan I have to help you grow.

You need to turn to those who care,
especially when you have a sad tale to share.

You are not to bear these burdens alone.
It's not good to let them build, for you're not made of stone.

We all have our times when we need help from above.
Don't be too proud to come to me for help, my love.

Your mother can be of help to you now
since she turned over her grudge, her head she did bow.

So keep your chin high, and know that I'm with you
to help keep you stable and be a special friend when you're
blue.

Keep on being cheerful, loving, and kind.
Don't let a few kicks, my love, leave you blind.

You're very special to me just the way you are.
A very nice little lady, please don't bottle yourself in a jar.

Come to me with your problems, seek help from those who
care.
This will help immensely, your burdens I will bear."

Say Yes to Jesus

You can't say no to Jesus;
I tried it, and I've failed.
You must be willing to sacrifice
in order not to be derailed.

"Your position should be very clear as to what to do with me.
If you'll truly accept me, I can set you free.

Free from all your worries for Carl and all your loved ones.
Free from all the boredom of growing old and aches and pains
in toes.

Free to live a new life with Christ, a life filled with my joy,
which you will not understand at all until my Spirit you do employ.

Casting your burdens upon the Lord is something you've heard
of, I'm sure,
but you haven't really gotten to know me or you'd know that
I'm your cure.

A cure for all that ails you, a beacon of light for thee,
a peace that passes all understanding, a calming of a roaring sea.

From this point, you'll begin to grow, to blossom like a flower.
You will learn of me and my Holy Spirit from whom you'll
receive new power.

Filled till overflowing, like a fountain of love, living life anew,
my Holy Spirit can do all this for you.

He is your connection, a special gift. There's a place in your heart to fill.
All you need to do is ask, and this new joy I will instill.

So come to me and tell me, pray that sinner's prayer.
Give yourself over to your Redeemer, then never fear. I'll always be there."

For Florence
Matthew 5-8

This came for a very special person who had a great deal to do with my realizing a deep personal need of Jesus and the Holy Spirit in my life.

"You are my pride and joy,
my love and joy you do instill.
This I appreciate from my child in Christ.
With you, my covenant I will fulfill.

In the light of day, you'll hear my call.
In the still of night, you'll feel my presence there.
There is a calling I have given you,
and you have responded, a responsibility you bear.

You have spread my Word through faith and deed,
evidence you've brought to bear by living the life you live.
That the Father, Son, and Holy Ghost are all important,
our presence in your life is what you have to give.

This life of yours pleases the Trinity,
for you listen closely for guidance, of this you are aware.
I'll always hold you close to me, for you are of me.
And I'll give you all you need to live and love and share.

Keep your gracious, grateful heart in tune,
for together we'll touch many lives to be sure.
There's nothing that pleases me more than to hear your praises,
for blessed are those who come to me whose hearts are pure.

Go spread your trophies at my feet, and I'll take care of them.
Don't fear or worry for your loved ones, for they are mine too.
They serve their Lord, some great, some small,
but even the least of their acts are important to me, 'tis true.

So praise me often, and I'll fill your soul.
This love, to you, I want to give.
Continue to pray for those near and dear.
You've served me well with this life you live."

Be More Like Christ
Colossians 3

As mothers, we sometimes forget who we are.
We think we are lord and master of our children.
We forget we're just caretakers for God,
and until he takes them home, we're just a fill-in.

The family is one of God's richest blessings.
Thank God he planned one for each of us.
It is a special love he gave us for our children,
a love to be nurtured and implanted into each one.

What a responsibility we carry; it's enough to scare you.
But God didn't intend for us to do this task alone.
He gave us a Friend to help us, an example to follow.
If done so, our children won't give us any reason to moan.

It's very difficult, you know, to follow this Friend's advice.
First there's our own selves, which must be forgotten.
For you can't decide what's best for your child
if it's done with your best interests in mind; that's kind of rotten.

God gave us his children to watch over.
He gave us also a very helpful guide;
our own Dr. Spock is our Bible, if we let it be.
I'm sure you'll agree that once read, its wisdom cannot be denied.

So just before you let out that scream of distress,
stop and think, *Now what would Jesus say?*
Now isn't that better? Just thinking of him has taken the venom
out of your tongue.
Now you're able to handle the situation, and besides, it's better
to do it Jesus's way.

Wisdom from God

I'm going to thank you, Lord, right from the start,
before I forget it and take for granted the wisdom you impart.

Grant me your wisdom, on this day,
to know how to talk, to be of some help, and then what to say.

I don't want to hurt or tear anyone down;
I only want to love and support people of this town.

Grant me courage to be bold when I speak,
to tell of my story without pride, to be chic.

Others need to know just what you can do;
I want to tell them but don't know how to.

If only I knew my Lord Jesus better,
I'd have some of these answers without this letter.

But thank you, Jesus, for through many a poem,
there have been misguided children brought back home.

Please keep them coming even though some resist;
I do really want them even if my sleep I must miss.

Now I'll ask you to guide me this day,
keep my family safe too, and remind me to pray.

During work, I forget to think of Jesus when I can;
my mind is on business, and I know it too is part of your plan.

Show me the way, show me what it is there I'm to do;
keep me happy there, Lord, for sometimes I become blue.

I know I'd much rather be home and be free,
free to share and to meditate when I please.

But that's a little selfish, and I know you have a plan,
so grant me your strength, Lord, and I'll do what I can.

Thirsting for God

"Oh, my God, my God, why must thou forsake me?"
Jesus spoke these words at a very lonely time in his life.
And yet we have many people today crying out in much the
same way.
Souls crying out to someone, somewhere, to save them from
this miserable life.

Many of God's people are searching for something they don't
know what,
a link somewhere maybe, a lifeline, their own little rope to
heaven.
This is a sad sight: God's people thirsting after the gospel,
trying to put some meaning into their life like a loaf of bread,
unleavened.

If you would liken this people to a loaf of unleavened bread,
until the gospel has been told and the thirst begins for more,
then the loaf begins to rise.
But to make the dough finer, it must be kneaded again.
Many truths are discouraged, many new thoughts unveiled,
and once more left to rise.

God can do this after you've accepted Jesus.
He can create a very helpful disciple.
Like bread dough, we must be kneaded.
Only until we are made into this finer person can we be disciples.

Many long hours are spent in kneading you into shape.
Many attributes you must have to be of help to God.
You can no longer belong to this earth and worldly things.
These must all become unimportant. From now on, you
belong to God.

He'll guide you if you'll let him right down the path to heaven.
He'll fill that void in the soul that you've been feeling.
You know now without a doubt what that lonely feeling was.
Now you'll have a new life full of love and good feelings.

Keep yourself on the right track. There are three things necessary to do that:
keep in touch with prayer, it's your lifeline to God;
learn how you're expected to live by the Word;
and then you must share the gospel with others whose souls are crying, "My God! My God."

Fallen Souls

The falling leaves are beautiful to me,
for they denote just how glorious life can be.

They fall with dignity upon the ground;
they're humble after they get there, I have found.

For they're trod upon by millions of feet;
they're raked and burned, for most feel they don't look so neat.

We don't want them lying around underfoot,
and yet just a short time ago, we'd drive around to look.

We'd all get in our cars to go out and see;
we just couldn't take in enough of their beauty.

In the spring, when the trees would bud,
we would recognize the miracle of God.

We all watch as the tiny leaves take shape,
wondering how many would hang on till late.

Yes, falling leaves are beautiful to me,
for they tell us a story, don't you see?

Each year from the start, they have their work cut out;
they labor hard for their God without a doubt.

They remain faithful and true right to the end,
for after they fall, they still have much to extend.

People are like this, if you care to stop and recall,
for our old folks too can be useful after they fall.

They may be infirm and difficult to take care of,
but the vast knowledge they have is what they can share.

We rake them into homes to get them out from under our feet,
but don't forget them, for visiting with old folks can be a real
treat.

The wisdom they can give is something to take in,
like the beauty of fall leaves blowing in the wind.

And then all at once they're gone, like the leaves of fall,
and everything looks barren, and we can no longer call.

We feel the cold of winter, and our hearts have a little ache,
but the sun in spring begins to warm us, and thank God for
our sake.

The trees begin to bud again, and once more, life begins.
Oh, thank you, God, for each fallen leaf and reassurance we'll
live again.

Reassurance

When will we see the progress we've been praying for?
I know you're there, for I've enough faith to believe.
The promises you made will be kept on your part.
This is for sure a time for renewal, not grief.

"You must be patient and not have so much doubt.
You can be sure I'll keep my covenant with you.
There will be a time when I will lift you up
to meet my hosts and find supreme joy. Please don't be blue.

Keep praying and loving, I know it's been strained.
The love you can feel, it's acting it out that has you trapped.
I'll help you over this hurdle if you'll listen to me.
I'll always tell you how and give strength, keep in contact.

Prayer, however little or big, is pleasing to me.
I appreciate the small, little sentences you shoot up.
I also know the problems and hear the long prayers.
Those you sometimes feel are selfish, I'll fill your cup.

I want very much to answer all your prayers,
and this I say to you,
keep on sending up the prayers and requests,
for this I promise is true.

The prayers will be answered despite your doubt,
for you and I have come a long way.
Turn your doubts into assurance and wait patiently,
for I heard and have a plan for each day.

The children will be all right and your husband too.
We'll all take care of them, my hosts and I.
You'll have your answer, and you'll see it someday.
Your loved ones are being cared for by and by."

Jesus Is the Way

Oh, Jesus, Jesus, Jesus, wellspring of my soul.
Keep me close to thee, Lord, through pruning keep me whole.

This I ever plead, we need thy kind touch
to keep us ever mindful, our Father gives so much.

Remember when our lives weren't filled with Christ;
oh, how dull! Life just seemed a sacrifice.

But now my fellow Christians, we have him in our hearts;
life is new, and each of us can have a new start.

Don't expect an easy road, it just won't be that way;
for the Lord must teach and train, so he's sure we're his to stay.

There's only one to worship now, all idols have been cast away;
we want it this way from now on, help us, Lord, we pray.

We know that each new day will bring a new temptation too;
so we ask you to give us wisdom to turn our thoughts to you.

This will reassure us that Jesus is by our side,
and all we have to do is ask and he will be our guide.

This is what he gives us now, life of joy to find,
and it's really there, you know; it's Jesus, he's one of a kind.

Love

Love really isn't blind, you know;
it goes hand in hand with a heavenly glow.

You really know what it's all about;
it's caring for someone without a doubt.

But it's more than that; it's seeing the good,
not getting upset with faults, and saying, "I'd change him if I
could."

It's caring enough to forget your own wants and desires;
it's wanting to give in ourselves what the other admires.

It's helping him with a project you don't even care for;
it's fun, and you'll enjoy because that's what you're there for.

A helpmate is more than a slave to this life;
it's helping your loved one to overcome his strife.

It's spreading yourself out to all the world,
to love and to care for the helpless and disturbed.

To give a lift with a smile on the street;
how pleasant to see the eyes of the old twinkle, my heart gives
a leap.

It's compassion, it's sharing, it's caring, it's love;
it's fulfilling as if seeing the heavenly dove.

What more could you ask than to be able to love?

Destructive Webs

A spider's web is a very intricate piece of art;
its many designs are beautiful, each and every part.

The scale is never out of proportion to the spider's size,
and that's as far as it goes, comparing webs of the wise.

Then we have webs of the not so wise,
the many people unable to see with their eyes.

We can't say their webs are beautiful or even an art,
for their many avenues are devious, each and every part.

Their webs also are meant to trap and snare;
their lives are so important that for others they don't care.

This self-centered person can ruin many lives, you see;
just by laying plans to work toward a selfish goal for the great me.

The people that are trapped are usually part of the family;
they love her, so it's easy to fall prey to devious planning.

This whole concept of self is so destructive, it's the one great
sin;
so examine your motives when laying your plans within.

Keep your mind on Jesus and your loved ones too;
this will help to forget what you thought you wanted to do.

Give up the self, and leave it behind
so we can start a walk of our own kind.

A walk that will take you to the right path,
a path that leads away from the webs of life we have.

Keep working and pushing self right out the door;
that's the only way Jesus can come through once more.

Sing Praises to His Name

I'll sing praises to his name, O Lord, Jehovah;
I'll sing praises to his name, O Lord, my King.

From whence comes my strength and my courage;
I'll sing praises to his name, O Lord, my King.

This I can assure you, his love he always gives;
not alone will you stand as long as he lives.

And he lives forever, throughout eternity,
so I'll sing praises to his name, O Lord, my King.

The blessings flow like water to fill a reservoir,
and this much I can say, they're given with love to restore.

With these blessings you'll find no strings attached;
they're given not because you earned them, only because you ask.

So seek it, the Lord your God, seek and you shall find;
this is a promise, don't ask me to define.

If the need is present and the desire to know,
this your Lord will lead you, he'll show you which way to go.

Just trust in your Redeemer, have faith that he will guide;
just hang in there with prayer, and his Word you will find.

Pick it up and read it through, it's clear now, isn't it?
Now remember where you read it, and remember what it said.

Now when you think of Jesus, sing praises to his name;
he'll hear and bless you, so thank him, your God and King.

A Way of Life

"It's only proper to tell each other your experiences. It's necessary for one another to grow and to learn. Before you feel great guilt for sharing your story, just remember all my work kept in secret cannot teach the world the ways of the Christ and of the Spirit.

You must share your thoughts especially when they are Spirit-filled. This is the only way of spreading a desire in another's heart to learn more of me. For once stirred, they will continue to thirst after righteousness. The hope and faith you have is very pleasing to me, as I have a plan in mind for you. And if you continue on the right path, you're going to fit in very nicely. My work and the understanding of what I want each of you to do is very important. Keep in close contact so you might begin to hear my calling and my directions. Remember, willing helpers I must have, I will not be calling to an unwilling helper too many times. It is a waste of time to ask repeatedly. Until there is a willingness to serve, I cannot touch you with the special joy that comes from doing my will with a willingness of heart.

Remember, I love you and am with you always. Don't hesitate to call on me for even the smallest things, as it pleases me to do for my children. Keep a faithful heart and your desires will come in good time."

Your loving Redeemer

A Prayer

We sing praises to your name, O Lord our God,
sing praises to his name ye heavenly hosts;
look up to the Lord your God with love and reverence.
Grant unto each of us full measure of the Holy Ghost.

This is how we sing; this is how we pray:

"O Lord God most high,
we lift our arms up to the sky.
Fill us, O Lord, we pray.
Send your Holy Spirit this day."

He'll take away the sin and doubt and fear;
he'll replace it with the love of Christ,
and from that moment on, Jesus will always be near.

My Friend

O Lord Jesus, what can I say
but thank you for this beautiful day?
Thank you, O Lord, for people everywhere.
Thank you, O Lord, for being willing to share.

There are some of your people who know you not,
but they haven't met you and still they're not forgotten;
you love us all as if we knew you quite well,
but it must sadden you to know some will go to hell.

I'm sure for those who pray that sinner's prayer,
a life in heaven they will have to share;
so for people everywhere, Lord, I will pray,
once they find you, their Lord, they're home to stay.

It's a long trip, for I know the road.
It's hilly and rocky, and we always seem to carry a load,
but with every step, the Lord Jesus is there
to help us carry our load and the burdens he'll bear.

Isn't it marvelous what knowing the Lord can do?
It seems to change the world, for you know he'll pull you through;
even those living in sin, we find we can love them too,
for they're God's children also, even though we don't like what
they do.

And given the right message, they too would change their ways.
Then to the Lord Jesus and Holy Spirit I'm sure they'd give praise.
So Lord Jesus, if you'll show us the way,
show us the path so we sinners won't stray.

Bind that old Satan, and keep him from our door,
never to trick us for our Lord we do adore.
Sometimes it happens that Satan enters in,
then we find ourselves falling right back into sin.

So continue to pray, read the word, and praise;
these will carry you through those difficult days.
Share your good message with those around you;
these four things are important to do. They all have value.

Your Friend Jesus
For Marilyn R.

"Without any hang-ups, there wouldn't be a need to turn to me,
and until you turn to me, I can't help you truly see.

Please ponder the circumstances of life without your Lord,
then call out the name of Jesus for he is to be adored.

Ask all the questions which have been plaguing your mind;
then relax, have faith, you'll see, the answers you will find.

Hope without faith won't do you a bit of good;
life without love of Christ means you've misunderstood.

The only way to see your Lord is through a deep love;
an abiding love of Christ will guarantee for you a heavenly dove.

This without a doubt is a friendship a Christian can't do without;
so practice praising your Lord Jesus, and don't feel silly for
what you're about.

It's a common practice among Christians, this praising the Lord;
it's the meaningful praise which brings the benefits to your door.

The Spirit will leap forward in its growth within;
then be careful you don't drive it back down with sin.

This is a very delicate situation which requires constant contact with your Lord,
and don't be surprised if Satan won't try to pull you back
through that door.

So keep a strong hold on everything you learn;
a close contact is needed so in the pit you won't burn.

A deep love of Christ will surely pull you through;
but many times it's hard, for in this world we become blue.

The fight is long and hard, but don't forget
there is a helpmate to see you through; have you met?"

To Be Spirit-Filled

Oh, heavenly Father, what more can I do
except ask for guidance from you?

Send to me this day
your Holy Spirit to guide my way.

Keep me ever mindful of his presence, I pray;
guide me, Holy Spirit, in everything I say.

To be a witness like John would be great,
but whatever your task for me, please state.

We all need to put you first, Lord Jesus, in our hearts;
to live to glorify God is what we're to impart.

In today's world, we have our work cut out for us
but with the Savior by our side to guide us.

This prayer is ever directed to claim your power,
and this we do, Lord, in order to have strength so we don't cower.

So when we rise each new day, we'll say thank you, Lord,
and now guide me this day so that my Lord will be adored.

Our task can be simple if we'll open ourselves to him;
just let Jesus take over and place the Holy Spirit within.

Then you'll be a witness that the Lord may respect;
he'll bring your work to you, to many people you can reflect.

You'll know just when and what to say,
for the Holy Spirit will guide each step of the way.

All you have to do is pray
for the guidance you'll receive each day.

A Calling

Oh, heavenly Father, how sweet the call,
that special touch that saves men from a terrible fall.

If only more would feel your touch;
isn't it sad they're blinded that much?

But you can undo what Satan has done;
you can lead them to a life of fun.

Then remembering back to the old life again,
how could I ever believe I could win?

I didn't know whether I was saved or not;
but you reassured me, and lost I'm just not.

So ever hereafter, I'll not doubt you, Lord;
I'll always remember just what I've been told.

Your words are a fountain of life, giving food;
how could I ever put it away? This I've never understood.

So keep me ever mindful of your presence within,
and life from hereon won't be full of sin.

For my sins you've forgiven with loving-kindness,
even when I didn't deserve it, I must confess.

Thank you, Lord, for saving my soul,
and now you'll ever be present as I work toward my goal.

Reassurance from God

"My promises you can be sure I will keep. My Word contains everything you need to know to be able to obtain them. Keep in close contact with your Savior at all times, and I will lead your spiritual life so you will be able to learn more of me. Don't hesitate to call on me for your needs, as this pleases me to be able to give to my children. It pleases you to be able to give to your children, and no man hath greater love than the Father, so how much more it should please him to give to you? Don't ever feel you are asking too much, for I will answer all your needs in due time as you will see when you begin to have faith that your prayers will be answered. Remember when you ask anything of me, always say thank you and believe it will be answered. I will not always answer in the way in which you feel it should be done but in the best way for all concerned. Many a covenant was made between God and man, and when you see the rainbow in the sky, please remember it is the sign that my covenant I will keep. Drink in its beauty as you watch the many hues blend together, and remember your part of the covenant. And then put no other gods before me. You say there are no idol worshipers today, but I say there are more than there were in my days on earth. Have you stopped to think that any material desire, when put before God, is an idol? Some men idol the money it takes to buy their material items. But I say to you, store your riches in heaven, for those who find their riches on earth will never have a single one in heaven. All men seeking glory on earth may find it, but woe to that man, for he shall receive none of heaven's benefits. So I beg of you to cast aside the world's desires and place in your hearts the will and desires of your Lord Jesus Christ. He alone can give you the riches that far surpass anything man could possibly conceive. This does not mean you must live the life of a hermit, permitting yourself nothing of this life at all. For everything upon this earth was placed there by God, your Father, for all to enjoy. But when it becomes so great a desire within you, you cannot do without it in place of what your Father would have you do, then you are plagued by idolatry. And I say this: fall to your knees and confess your sin and ask the Lord to forgive it and to remove this desire from your heart, for to be sure, Satan has placed it there, and no one can follow Satan and the Father at the same time. For you shall love one and hate the other or hate one and love the other. All in all, you will become torn apart and miserable. Please cast your burdens upon me, for I am your Savior and your Light of the world. Seek ye first the kingdom of God, and you shall have all the riches that will satisfy your soul. In Jesus's name, you shall be blessed."

A Heavenly Call

Oh, Lord Jesus, come be my guest;
and now do I really pass the test?

Is there a time limit that I must go by?
And if I don't make it, shall I die?

Some of these questions must plague some minds,
if only they could find their answers in time.

Keep calling them, Lord, so just maybe they'll hear;
then maybe they'll listen with a discerning ear.

This I pray will be their dream:
to become a friend of Jesus, a true Christian, so it seems.

Just maybe someday we'll see a transformation;
that would be wonderful if it happens to all creation.

I can see a chance, a glimmer of hope,
because surely they're searching in their own little boat.

Keep pulling them in, Lord, all those wandering Jews;
and someday soon, they're all going to choose.

But I wait for the day when they all return home;
to see what will happen, will we all be called home?

It's not too clear just what John saw on that island;
but we'll keep trying, and through insight, we'll plan.

To be alert would be helpful, even so we must know;
we must recognize our Lord when he does show.

There will be false gods that will lead many astray;
I just hope not too many, and this I will pray.

I'll even pray for those led astray,
that before it's too late, they'll repent and come back to stay.

It's ever a mystery, and so it should be;
it's better we don't understand everything we see.

And what will it matter once we're up there?
When we come home, we simply won't care.

There will be rejoicing and singing to do,
and of course whatever the Lord will ask of you.

So just don't worry and fret at all
because it's going to happen, that heavenly call.

Praise Him

Oh, heavenly Father, this I must pray,
keep everything on an even keel today.

I don't know why days go this way;
that's why I feel I must pray.

Satan seems to be at his best some days;
that is why we should continually give Jesus praise.

O Lord, help me this day to understand why,
and I know that you'll answer by and by.

And someday soon, when I'm close as I can be,
I won't have to worry about Satan playing tricks on me.

But in the meantime, while I'm struggling to come close,
I'll just keep binding Satan and praising ye heavenly hosts.

So thank you for the privilege, Lord, of praising your name,
and blessing my family in Jesus's name.

I feel you have given much more than I can return,
so please let me thank you for gifts I could not earn.

I'll try even harder to be your willing helper,
but I do need your touch often to reassure you're my keeper.

You've always helped me out of some most difficult situations,
and for this I'm grateful, and I'd like to shout it to the nations.

But I know I must wait for your wisdom and guidance,
for I'm not always able to separate flesh from heavenly guidance.

And to witness for Christ, one must be quite sure what to say,
so I'll wait for the Holy Spirit to guide what I'm to say.

If that's not enough, then I'll pray to give more;
take my mind, heart, and soul, and show me the door.

I'm willing, O Lord, I pray you'll use me today;
and keep that old Satan out of my way.

Binding Satan

Forgive me, Lord Jesus, this I pray,
and please keep me humble throughout this day.

How easy it would be for me to slip and fall;
I must fight Satan at every call.

He tempts me many times a day
if I forget for a shield to pray.

I ask for it every day that I remember,
and this is a lifeline that Satan can't sever.

So keep me ever mindful of the need to pray,
whether at home, at work, or even at play.

"It's so important, and it takes only a few words.
Just carry on a conversation with Jesus, and if heard,

Satan can't get through as long as your mind's on the Lord.
For he will flee at the mention of the blood of the Lord.

Satan can't win
when there's the presence of the Spirit within.

Oh, he'll tempt you almost every day,
but don't fall into his trap, just remember to pray.

Satan will tempt you with fear, envy, and doubt,
but don't you believe him, you're saved without a doubt.

If you've come far enough to understand what I've said,
then you can be sure I have a spot for you to rest your head.

An eternal pillow is waiting for you,
and just you believe that the Lord Jesus will pull you through."

A Special Baby

Little Lord Jesus, how sweet the babe;
the little Lord Jesus that God hath made.

Truly a human baby was born,
a baby which came to this earth to warn.

A baby of love filled with a special joy,
but human enough that he'll play with a toy.

Little Lord Jesus, how sweet you are;
even the wise men came from afar.

Oh, to have seen such a wonderful sight,
to have knelt and prayed right there by his side.

How lucky they were, those first visitors;
how could they know he would cause such a stir?

A sweet little boy child destined for fame,
an everlasting hero to those who will claim.

How great God's love must have been for Mary, his mother,
to receive from her God such an honor.

So this year, when we celebrate a birth of a King,
open our hearts, let us praise and joyfully sing.

Oh, how we love that sweet little babe,
and how we thank him for all that he gave.

A vision he's given of eternal peace within,
a vision of a world free from all sin.

An everlasting promise has come our way;
now let's open our hearts, kneel down, and pray.

Spend Time with Jesus

Jesus, Jesus, how I love that name;
the world was surely blessed when you came.

With all your heavenly ardor and hue,
this world will never again be the same because of you.

If only we all could love you as we should,
wouldn't this be a lovely world if we just would?

The scriptures tell us how and even more;
all we have to do is read them, but some would say it's a bore.

What better way to spend free time
than to come in contact with Jesus, it's just sublime.

When I think of all the years and what I've missed,
I feel very thankful that I'm now on his list.

All sins forgiven, that's what he says;
and you better believe it because that's why he gave that life
of his.

The Trip

Heavenly Father, am I to go?
Will you be able to help each of us know?

Will all the girls be able to go?
And will it be exciting, Lord? I hope so.

This little trip I've been longing for,
feeling maybe I'll have a special chore.

Will I be urged to go forward or not?
And what will it be for? If I am, don't let me stop.

Grant the strength I'll need to get me through this day,
and I know that everyone there will want to pray.

I pray for the girls going along today,
for they're excited too and need to pray.

I pray for the speaker of the day
and pray that we'll all understand what she's to say.

I pray for the women putting this on;
I pray their organization will grow to be strong.

If there are any more reasons I should pray,
I pray that you'll bring them to mind today.

I know not of this speaker or what she might bring,
but I'm sure, if she is your agent, then we'll all want to sing.

And just maybe there will be another poem
to tell of the day's happenings when I get home.

God's Powerful Hand

I saw bodies healed and lives being saved,
and I thank God for all he gave.

He healed a friend, I'm sure he did,
and I even helped as the others did.

We all said a prayer, and what do you know,
another body was made whole.

What a wonderful sight as many wept tears of joy,
for now they have been released from Satan's ploy.

For only Satan will harm us and make us sick,
for God is love; he wants us whole for his sake.

He uses old Satan's powerful ills
to show us the way to a life of his will.

How marvelous the Holy Spirit at work,
turning fear into power, and it really does work.

I saw many a poor soul claiming health for their own,
and I wept tears of love for others I didn't even know.

I saw women slain in the Spirit and given a peace;
oh, how wonderful, I sat in awe of his powerful release.

I even felt it as I stood under her hands;
I very near fell as the blessings began.

Likewise, my friend weaved under the power,
and I can't deny how great is his power.

Praise God evermore, and in reverence I stand,
a firm believer and receiver of what God has planned.

God's Gift

Oh, heavenly Father, how I love thee
and this your universe as far as the eye can see.

But greater still will be the new world, I feel,
where there won't be any sickness; everyone will be healed.

But even so, Lord, what I saw the other day
will always be remembered and shows that the Lord will lead
the way.

Christmas is upon us, and this time of the year,
it's really special; Lord Jesus, help us hear.

Hear beyond the gifts and celebrations
to remember a babe and give him celebration.

Sometimes we get so wrapped up with our cheer,
we forget just why Christmas is really here.

Think of that Christ child years ago,
that little Christ child who didn't have anywhere to go.

When time for his birth, he picked the right place,
for that's how God wanted it, but Joseph tried just in case.

God did the planning all the way this time,
from the manger of hay to the star in the sky.

And even the angels played their part;
just a few knew of the birth at the start.

But the news spread rapidly, for in days of old,
I think God had to help it along so the story would be told.

Thank you, God, for the gift you have given;
thank you, God, for now I can get to heaven.

Let the Spirit Lead

Oh, Lord Jesus, it has happened again. The questions have come,
I feel once more, this round, the Holy Spirit has won.

If only I could have stayed for a longer talk,
but it wouldn't have worked out. I had to walk.

Your Spirit always knows best, and this I say,
he's guided quite well all this day.

The kids have been filled with love,
and even Don had control with help from above.

I pray it will continue, and please bless each one;
this family is trying, and the Holy Spirit has won.

There's a peace within, I'm sure you can see it;
and it's there to stay, for the Lord said so be it.

Satan can't win in this house anymore,
for our Lord Jesus has shown him the door.

We're clinging to his Word from this moment on,
and no one will deter us from singing our song.

Through God's Holy Spirit, we'll do his will,
and no one can alter what God does instill.

Our God, you come first, and this we do say;
our final commitment will be on resurrection day.

We're going home then in a special way,
home to our Lord Jesus, there to stay.

It couldn't be a more perfect dream,
and you'll only make it through Jesus, this perfect dream.

A Time to Reflect

It's almost time for that babe to appear to us;
just as poorly as he can possibly seem to us.

Yet wise men of old found him much to behold,
and even the shepherds were amazed when told.

This beautiful story is quite timely right now,
and when I think of how humble, my head I do bow.

Think of the innkeeper, how sad he must have been
when he said to the strangers, "I have no room at the inn."

And yet little did he know, God planned it that way,
or it might not have been such a very special day.

Special or not, it's the Christ child we need,
and this time of the year seems to plant a special seed.

It seems to fester and grow as his day comes near.
When we realize it's God's love in us, it's already here.

Oh, for that spirit all year long,
that special warmth makes you want to sing a song.

A song of love for a baby dear,
and I pray for each of you he soon will appear.

For if you see Christ, then rest assured,
then you're really special, for it says in the Word.

"Never fear if you don't, but keep trying always.
Cast your burdens on me, and praise when you pray."

A Teaching

"The expression of love and joy can be ever present in your lives. There is never any doubt in the Father's love for you, but at times, you can say of yourselves, 'I doubt because I'm not really sure because it hasn't been proven to me to meet my satisfaction.'

But consider the consequences of that doubt. With only one little doubt, Satan can enter in and take hold of a fear you might have about yourself and pull you right into sin. For that doubt will fester and grow, and you'll find yourself doubting even more about other things you thought you had put aside. It isn't the sins that result that will pull you away. Oh yes, the guilt of those sins will have some effect, but don't you see it's the doubt in the first place that hurts you? I can think of no other thing that could destroy your faith as fast as a growing doubt that says to me that I have not been honest with you. You know that this could not be so. I could only speak honestly, and when you read in my Word, that I am the truth, the light, and the way, you surely cannot think that I would be dishonest in my dealings with your spiritual life. Please don't cast me aside by doubting. Don't you know that once I have you, I will not let you go? I will continue to bring you back into that life of spiritual joy. But you cannot continually put me aside and not want to give up eventually. Once you give up, I cannot help you. When you deny me, I must leave you if you do not repent. Please remember to call out to me with every doubt and fear. You can cast Satan out, and the fear will disappear if you will remember to call on my name. I will always be present as long as you call to me. Strive to move closer to your Christ, and never forget I am in you as the Father is in me and I in him. Your recognition of this is a first step to a closer relationship with me. Praise will help you and definitely be a source of joy for you. Continue to pray and never cease to praise my name."

God's Guidance

"With tears in her eyes, a child's calling to me.
Please help me, O Lord, help me to see.

And help her I will, only this she must do:
keep open my line of contact with prayer so I might get through.

It so often happens that young ones forget,
then truths I can't show them if on me their mind is not set.

Continual contact that is the key. Never forget that I love thee.
Satan will test you, and try as he might, the closer you get, the
harder he'll fight.

But Satan can't win if you continue to pray.
Just bind that old enemy, and send him away.

Keep your faith strong, believe in me always and never fear.
Satan can't harm you as long as I'm here.

Oh, the enemy will try to fool you with tricks he might play,
but I'm always there to change the course of events if you pray.

Remember, your Bible is where you will learn,
as well as experiences in life, for they'll keep your faith firm.

Never fail to thank me for that answered prayer,
even before you ask it, as if you know I'm right there.

Continue to share with those who feel as you do.
This will help you learn and raise your spirits if blue.

Never feel lost from this moment on,
for now I'm with you, a true friend to lean on.

I'll never fail you, and I speak only the truth.
And don't forget prayer and praise, for that's how I get through."

Transcending Love

It brings tears, Lord, for I love him so,
that little babe of long ago.

With shining light about his head
and a stable manger for his bed.

How beautiful a sight, I must admit;
God knew just where he must fit.

A humble birth he doth proclaim;
not even we can admit the same.

He had no pride that we know;
only God's love did he show.

How wonderful to have a teacher as he,
who says God loves even me.

Grant me the patience, Lord, to show this love too;
so this family can have Jesus's love transcending through and
through.

The Glory of God

And so it was that the Christ child was brought to bear and was laid in a manger. Praise God and all the heavenly hosts for this is the coming of the Messiah. Then in the fields of old Judea, the shepherds were biding their sheep. Little did they know what a glorious experience they were about to have. When all of a sudden, the brilliance of day was about them, and an angel of the Lord spoke, saying, "Follow the star and worship your King." How glorious was the night, how wonderfully bright were the heavens that night. Even the wise men were made aware of the importance of the night, and how much more we should glorify God by praising this babe of long ago and giving homage to his almighty presence this day. Bow your head and give thanks for your Lord, and remember the humility under which he was brought to you. Take yourself to him in this same way. Never to think you are his one and only disciple on this earth, for surely you will be wrong. Praise your God and King, praise his holy name. Never more shall this earth be lost as it was before Christ. But as it was predicted, it did come to pass. The glory of God was and still is our Lord and King, our guidance in the world forevermore. Eternity will be ours only if we ask and praise his Holy One.

Our Sins Forgiven

Oh, Lord Jesus, how miserable I can be,
especially when I might have offended thee.

"Don't worry, my child, the sin is forgotten.
For you've been forgiven, or have you forgotten?

When these little errors come up,
just be sure to ask that I refill your cup.

For this is the important part of repenting
so you'll be in a position to start mending.

Your spirit will need to be uplifted.
For you to be of service, you must be gifted.

When my children fall out of favor,
their spirit is damaged. It's not what I gave you.

It must be repaired, so you must ask again.
Yes, repent but be sure to ask to be refilled again.

You need your gifts to be of service to me.
You must use them if you expect more of me.

The more you give out, the more you'll take in.
And when you're in service, you're almost free from sin.

It's when we lose sight of the ultimate goal
that trouble begins, and you begin to build your ego.

This building of ego, I cannot permit,
for while ego is present, there is no room for me to fit.

So keep your eyes upon Jesus as much as you can.
Then you won't have to worry, self won't fit into your plan."

Our Gracious Lord

Surely, Lord Jesus, you'll not miss.
If there is a blessing, it will be bliss.

These many times I've awakened to say,
"Please, Lord Jesus, what is it today?"

Is there a poem or a song in the air?
If I'm amiss, this I could not bear.

I only want to serve you the best that I can.
But there are times when I feel I mess up the plan.

Forgive me, Lord Jesus, if I've been amiss.
Too sleepy, too groggy, to write such as this.

"Don't fret, my child, if there have been times.
I just wait till you're ready or use other's signs.

My work will be done, you can be sure.
If you were not able, there were others who were.

I know the flesh is weak and how much you can take.
I'm sure you also know I won't overload you for your sake.

For when my children are tired, I give them a lift.
Haven't you noticed when doing my work you always feel fit?

I'll not let you tire when doing my work,
for it's too easy for Satan to attack when you're not mentally alert.

Go with my blessing back to your bed.
Don't ever feel you've messed up instead.

I'll do what I must to accomplish my end
and thank my Father in heaven for being able to bend."

The Angel

I praise you, Lord Jesus, if this vision was of thee;
and if it was, did the angel have a message for me?

I come to recall the light was there;
the angel in white and gold was brought to bear.

I saw it, I know now, through my mind's eye,
and praise God from above and heavenly hosts on high.

So Father, my question is now,
what does this mean? My head's too thick to understand how.

"The angel you saw was truly of me.
You saw it, believe it, let it comfort thee.

Don't fear its meaning or what it might say.
You'll know the why and wherefore someday.

Keep in touch, for there will be more.
I'm just beginning to open a door.

Keep praying and praising, you know that it's true.
When you're doing this, Satan can't get through.

Don't fear Satan's trickery anymore.
For I'm with you always, your Lord to adore.

So lay down your head, but be alert from now on.
There will be more visions as my message goes along.

Special words will come sometime in the future.
These will be something your heart can nurture."

Praise God on high, his angels surround him.
Praise Lord and Spirit, I love each and all of them.

Casting Out Idol Worshipping

"If by the time the visions complete
there is still dirt to be swept from your feet,

then there is real trouble awaiting you,
and this trouble won't see you through.

There is misery in what lies ahead,
and it won't do to cover up your head.

There won't be any place to hide,
and an unfaithful servant, I can't abide.

So remember your place is at my feet,
serving your Lord, not worrying what you'll eat.

This idol worshiping can't go on.
You know and I know just what should belong.

So rinse away the dirt from your feet.
Then come to me and take your seat.

There is one here for you in my kingdom above.
And these will be saved for the ones who show love.

But still you have a job to do,
before you can come to your home in the blue.

A servant of mine is helpful and kind.
Remember that when dealing with mankind.

Don't let anger drive the Spirit away.
You've got to remember to continually pray.

Forgiveness is love, and you must forgive,
in order to breathe freely and begin to live.

This is a message I had to impart.
I'm sure if you study, you'll find your start.

Remember I'm with you, so call on me.
Don't be ashamed to get down on bended knee.

Go to your room and give it a try.
You've got to surrender all if I'm to supply.

I'll give you everything you'll need,
to live an obedient life. My word to heed.

You'll find it easier than you think.
Just remember, look back and think.

Do you recall the sinful life you led?
Don't recall it with desire for it to return, it's dead.

Your life is new,
and your desires should be too."

The Vision
John 12:13-21

I saw a man's head fall back, but I knew him not.
And Jesus said it was as before,
"You can't understand it as there will be more to come.
But it's also part of that opening door.

Each little part will come by itself.
Don't doubt it or leave anything out.
It must be recorded so you can put it together,
for there will be more without a doubt.

There should be a sign of reassurance to you,
a sign of a blessing that's yet to come.
For what lies ahead may frighten you.
So don't try to figure where it all comes from.

You certainly will understand when your Father is through
and all the visions are complete,
there will be verses for guidance given to you.
Just be alert, for I will not repeat.

I'll see that you rise to copy it down,
for I'll not let you rest till you do.
I can't give you more until each peace is there,
or it won't be worth anything to you.

Remember the name of the man in your mind.
Check it out in your news report too.
Never again doubt that it wasn't of me.
You saw it when it happened, his last breath was due.

It's opening slowly, and it must be that way.
You could not comprehend it all at once.
Each vision, each verse must be studied,
so be patient and don't be frightened of what's to come."

Understanding

There was no vision last night as I recall.
So Lord, what is it this time, an explanation of it all?

"It's not finished, it will take a long time.
There isn't anything but guidance this time.

Keep watching your news and checking it out.
You'll find I am right without a doubt.

There wasn't any vision this time at all.
So believe me when I say I will call.

I'll call when I need you, and you'll hear.
You'll know when there is a vision. It will appear.

Keep watching for signs of my coming someday.
You find most in the paper today.

Matthew 5 is important to you.
Study it again through and through.

Keep in touch while you study it through.
I'll give you some insight on the beatitudes.

The visions will come again in good time.
And the man wasn't right, so don't give him your time.

I would prefer you to give time to me in prayer,
as many of your preachers of today don't have what you have.

They won't understand why you do and they don't have it, so they must say it can't be, and that's why—because it's their ego which keeps them from it.

So believe me when I say
this is of me this day."

The Beauty of it All

O Lord Jesus, thank you for this new day.
Thank you for the sunshine of yesterday.

The trees, though barren are beautiful too.
And even the sky was an azure blue.

The beauty of it all is much to comprehend;
just think, God made all this with his hands.

Beauty, beast, and birds of the sky;
how glorious and precious, we all should cry.

"Now give of yourself so you might be
as beautiful and precious as God meant you to be.

This world must have its sin and shame.
But children of God look forward to the world without blame.

So give what you can to this world right now,
and when you get to heaven, you can take your bow.

Praise God up above, all ye creatures below.
Praise Father and Son and Holy Ghost."

Walking
& Talking with Jesus

O Lord Jesus, walk with me this day;
let each and every one I touch see God, I pray.

Help me to be a more loving servant of thee,
to help with your plan without questioning thee.

Praise be to God, how wonderful is he,
to love such a lowly person as me.

O Lord, be part of my life every minute;
don't let me falter and mess up within it.

The love that you show is the love I must have;
I want to give others what I have.

Lord, watch over us all this windy day;
don't let any of us blow away.

Keep us in touch with a nudge from above;
keep us ever mindful of his wonderful love.

O Lord, my God, be with me this day;
be with each and every member of my family, I pray.

The Essence of Life

O Father in heaven, hear my plea;
help each and every member of my family to see.

They all need to know their Savior better,
so when their time comes, they won't need a letter.

I pray each day for that Christian family now;
I feel I must even though I know I'll have it somehow.

You'll see to that for you've promised you would,
and Gerry and Lelia know what happened and understood.

Oh, how marvelous it will someday be,
to be open to share what we feel and believe.

To learn and grow together someday,
like it should have been from the first we started on our way.

I've ask for so much, and you've been so good;
you, Lord, have given and always understood.

When I came crying and pleading to you,
you always opened the door that I could see through.

I praise your existence and thank the Father above,
for all the special care he's given, that special love.

I know I don't know much about him,
but someday soon, I'll share with him.

Praise God up above and the heavenly hosts,
Lord Jesus Christ, and the Holy Ghost.

Praise them, I will, for each one to me
is the essence of life and the way to eternity.

The Cross

O Lord Jesus, you took it away that day on the cross.
All my sin and shame, you bore
All for the day when I'd understand
What, Lord Jesus, you have in store.

You gave up your life to show me the way.
You gave it all up for me;
O Lord Jesus, it's hard to comprehend,
Why you would do it just for me.

Circles were drawn, lots were cast,
Jealousy and hatred abound;
Around your feet, they gathered there,
Some just waited without even a sound.

Then came the words you spoke that day
Which proved beyond doubt who you were;
The final breath was taken, and life left you.
The centurion pierced your side to be sure.

How cruel we are with our earthly games
That drove that spear even deeper;
O Lord, how precious was the blood you shed,
You truly are our keeper.

Thank you, Lord, that it didn't end,
When in that tomb you were lain;
Thank you, Lord, from the bottom of my heart,
That thou didst rise again.

The Plan

"Some time ago, I gave to you a plan;
A plan to follow if you could understand.

I planned to nurture you along;
Till one day soon, you would be ready to follow.

If this plan is realized,
Then there will be others to scrutinize.

Keep your faith alive by me;
See that you worship One in Three.

There isn't any one part of me you can deny;
Just to worship one would be wrong in my mind.

You have to give it balance, your worship and study;
To delve into one aspect would be the wrong way to study.

Give credit to those around you for what you've learned;
And praise God the Father you've been able to discern.

Many so-called prophets will give of their beliefs;
You must know by the Word so you won't suffer grief.

Turn to your friends when you need to share;
They will be the ones who will really care.

Don't suffer alone when you can talk it out;
It will help to talk and sort things out.

If left to yourself, you'll find it too hard today;
It's for people like you that I've had others forge the way.

Most people have fallen away from the beliefs first taught;
They have given way to false beliefs, and they forgot whom
they had sought.

Don't give up your quest to understand;
It's all part of my emerging plan.

This must come someday to you;
And you must have the friends to see you through.

No one could travel this road alone;
You'll have a family I'll call my own.

Someday the chain of habit will break;
You'll have to try hard for your children's sake.

Believe your Father, he'll not let you down;
Someday you'll make it, you'll wear your crown.

I know how you suffer when you've fallen short;
And believe me, I forgive, and I'll give you support.

Keep looking for my guidance in all that you do;
So far this week this, you've been able to do.

I've not required much as you know;
For you've needed rest and time to grow.

You'll have your time to rest when you need it;
You can't do my work when tired, for you'd be defeated.

Cast out your problems and turn to me;
Worship in full the One in Three."

That Special Rapport

Lord Jesus, Lord Jesus, I'm calling your name,
for on this day I feel so strange.

I'm praying, Lord Jesus, for mercy and love;
I'm praying, Lord Jesus, for the touch of the dove.

A sign I'll not ask of you this day;
you owe me nothing, just let me humbly pray.

To stay in your presence and reach for the warmth,
I can't understand how I could have lost out.

I'm working and trying, Lord Jesus, so very hard;
I must find the answers so you can be proud.

Proud once again that I'm under your care;
listening and doing, that rapport that's so rare.

Oh yes, Lord Jesus, I really do care.

A Gift

Lord Jesus, there was no vision;
I have already made this decision.

"You're right, there wasn't any today.
But you still must remember to pray.

The talk you had was helpful to you.
And talks like this will help you through.

I've given to her the same as you.
Compare your notes, don't question if it's true.

Study my words through and through.
Believe me, I am working through you.

Don't ever feel I let you down.
Not one of my children can fall to the ground.

I keep close watch and my angels do too.
We're always close by even when you feel apart from us.

Don't worry about this door that's opening to you.
It's opening to Gerry too.

You'll be able to compare and see what's next.
You'll know what I mean, you've passed the test.

I won't ask any more of you than you can handle.
Don't fear that your family might be hurt by scandal.

You certainly know this about me by now.
I'd never hurt you. I wouldn't know how.

Please tune your ear to hear what I say.
Yes, discernment you must have. To achieve it, just pray.

Visions will come and scripture and guidance along the way.
There will be help for you now from day to day.

Pull yourself together, and stay calm about this.
Someday soon you'll all feel the bliss.

I'll not leave you even for a minute.
There wouldn't be any reasoning in it.

You must read your Bible, and be alert too.
Keep that line open so I can get through.

Praise Father, Son, and Holy Ghost.
Alleluia to the heavenly hosts."

Matthew 5

Heavenly Father, what is it this time?
Is it more of the sublime?

Can I count on guidance today?
About the visions, what do they say?

"You'll have to wait more patiently.
You're not ready to really see.

You must be taught each step of the way.
Then someday you'll be informed in a special way.

This is further guidance for you today.
It will require study, be sure to pray.

Now you have help in learning of me.
And don't worry, for discernment will come to thee.

You'll learn rather quickly, for others have forged the way.
But I'll need your time, so rather free you must stay.

Pick up the book of Matthew 5,
and read what it says inside.

Read carefully and closely, along with prayer.
I'll open up avenues you never knew were there.

This will take time, and you don't have much of that.
But what you do have, you'll need to find the facts.

Then remember what I've said in the past.
You've written it down so you won't have to ask.

I've been teaching you through your poems each day.
Read them over, it will help open the way.

Learning takes time, for each vision you see
will need to be nurtured, and then pray to me.

Keep your faith strong, just trust in the Lord,
your Keeper, Redeemer, and Savior adored."

Casting Out Doubt

"You are going to hear many of my words, so keep an open ear.
I can only work through those who are willing to hear.

Isn't it possible that each line you write is really not of me?
But if you pray and ask to know, I'll not desert thee.

You have been worried about this gift and ask many questions of late.
I tell you this, don't fret anymore, just write and appreciate.

Commas and periods and good English you have learned, but never doubt my Word.
I've said it before and I'll say it again, to doubt your gift is absurd.

Write down each urging, and remain open to my call.
I'll not let you wrong anyone. This kind of plan I would stall.

When you have learned more of me, you'll notice I'm not misleading you.
There will be words and poems to give, and you must have faith to see you through.

Each writing may have a message that someone that day will need to hear.
If you give of your poems reading, I'll guide them to the proper listening ear.

Have faith and believe, don't doubt yourself so.
You have so little confidence in yourself, and this must not continue to grow.

True, I want you to rely on me and not to become proud,
but you must believe what you believe and then don't begin
to doubt.

Each word you write I know you question,
but there must be faith before perfection.

So praise your Father for your gift and no more questions of him.
Cast out your disbelief of it and concentrate on serving him.

You're doing fine, and don't despair.
You'll not be compared with Jean Dixon's style and flare.

God works differently, you see.
All his workers must have humility.

So go about your day with care and ease.
Don't forget for one moment I want to please.

I'll give you much more than what you have and much more
faith too.
You'll have discernment, but that's not all. You'll have a deeper
faith to see you through."

Patience

"The scriptures should be studied through and through.
This must be a regular requirement of you.

The Word is important, it gives you my truths.
Keep digging in spite of distractions by youths.

Your world isn't private anymore like it was.
More boldness is needed, don't fear for those you love.

You'll not hurt their progress if they see you pray.
It just might be remembered by them in a very special way.

Someday when they need help from their mother,
someday when everything looks black, they'll wonder.

Wonder what Mom got from all that praying,
why it meant so much as an everyday thing.

Special remembrances from their past will be a big help
because it's not very pleasant to fight Satan without help.

You'll be able to tell them much more someday soon
when your Christian home begins to bloom.

There'll be contacts with each other in a special way.
One they'll remember was seeing you pray.

You awoke expecting another vision, I know.
The brightness of the night sort of fooled you though.

Be patient, they'll come when the time is right.
First you must learn, it's slow, it's a fight.

A fight for the time, the quiet you need.
You'll grow in spite of the rush, for I've planted a seed.

I'll nurture that seed and help it along.
Whenever you need a lift, sing one of your songs.

You must get to work on those songs once again.
To just let them lie idle would be a sin.

I know you are busy and there are many tasks to do,
but keep pressing for time of your own, just for you.

Now rest is important, you need your sleep too.
So lay down your head and think all this through."

Thank you, Lord Jesus, for poems such as these.
I can wait for the visions now more patiently.

A Blessed Family

Oh, come, Lord Jesus, be thou my guest;
bless this family as others have been blessed.

"You wouldn't want another family's type of blessing.
You will have your own as each family is questioning.

Each Christian family is blessed by me
to be a special family group, very unique and free.

Free from a label that might be given by others,
for this only tends to stifle the creativity, it smothers.

You must be flexible as a family unit.
To be cast in a form would be wrong for those in it.

When blessings are given to families as a Christian unit,
there is much work accomplished within it.

Each family is able in their own comfortable way,
to see to the spreading of the gospel each day.

If all were the same,
my message would be in vain.

So ask for a blessing from your Father above.
Ask for a deeper, more abiding love.

He will surely bless your family if you ask,
but don't limit him to an impossible task.

To ask to be the same as one other family,
it's not what you'll receive, so take what he's planning.

Be thankful and glad for just what you have.
There will surely be more for your family to have."

Games God Plays

As the end of the month draws nigh,
I haven't seen anything even when I look toward the sky.

"The heavens will open to you someday,
and you'll understand the games I seem to play.

Nothing is clear right now to you,
but you have the faith to see you through.

You know now not to doubt.
You also know patience must also rule out.

So each time you ask for a sign,
immaturity rushes in, and you're past a Christian of this kind.

I do know your heart and all your needs.
They'll be supplied even before you do good deeds.

You'll have everything you need when you go forth,
but first you'll need preparation and my Word shall support.

Cling to the Word and go forth prayed up within.
Remember to take guidance from my Spirit within.

You'll witness someday without a doubt,
you have already, so don't fret how you look from without.

You live a cleaner life, that you know.
And though many thoughts and attitudes need changing,
you're still ready to go.

Just a closer contact is needed right now.
And I know you're busy and asking just how.

All day long, you converse with me,
so pray in this way whenever you see things that need words
from thee.

I will show you more soon enough.
Don't get too anxious, or you'll read in too much.

I will give answers someday of my own.
I'll not permit you to dream up your own.

You know how easy it is to be wrong every time.
You've misinterpreted many a rhyme.

You'll see clearly what's expected of you,
when I'm eventually through.

The visions will come in due time
and more explanations and confirmation in rhyme.

Care for yourself, be healthy and alert.
Eat proper foods and get your rest so you'll be alert.

Taking care of your body, as your minister says, as well as your
soul,
it's very important, for to do my work, I want you healthy and
whole.

Praise your Father for the poem of today.
Do it in a joyful and prayerful way."

A Message from God

"Oh yes, you will hear many words. Words of assurance and guidance, words of love and concern. You will be lifted up as you continue to look up and praise his name. Only leave everything that troubles you at my feet, for I am your answer to many problems you are trying but can't possibly solve. The teaching, "Child help thyself," is embedded deep within you and has gotten to be a source of trouble. For when trying to solve the little problems, you fail to think to give them to me and leave them there.

Balance is a needed aspect in your life. A good program and set of rules in the home will do more to instill love, peace, and security to your family than criticism can ever do. Remember to leave your current problem with me and ask for my guidance about each little thing so I can work this contest into a pleasant and spiritually motivated way of life in your home.

Believe me, Don will catch on and fall right into place as he sees your lead and realizes its worth. Create peace by praise. Praise me when things aren't going so well. You learned this lesson long ago. Remain in my presence this day and you shall be at peace."

Your loving Redeemer,

Jesus Christ, your Lord.

What Does Criticism Matter

"What does criticism matter,
you're not going to fall.
It can't take you from me.
It's not of the Lord at all.

Remember, to take it is good,
for if persecuted for me,
you'll find a special reward,
a place next to me for thee.

Don't lose sight of the ultimate goal.
I know you're weary and tired of work.
And too, you need to share.
It can't all be gained by reading a book.

You know what it is to be hurt.
You know what it is to work.
Now you're learning what it is to negotiate
and raise a family outside the church.

They'll not be there forever,
and you'll see the way open up.
When it's the right time, I'll call.
They'll open their hearts, and I'll fill their cup.

Don't be impatient. It's never good.
They'll come to me, rest assured.
I've given each of them a free will,
but with what they see in you, they'll be stirred.

I've taken you from the group, as you know,
and now I believe you understand why.
They are ahead and you can't travel too fast.
Soon you'd be confused and wouldn't know why.

You'll see it all in your own good time.
Don't fail to be patient and wait on me.
It could be a beautiful experience,
a special reassurance of your own from me."

Trusting God

Oh, Lord Jesus, what is thy bidding?
Can I understand thy call?
Am I going to receive a vision?
Is it all over? Will there be nothing at all?

"You've been patient, and this has been good.
You've watched and waited but not pleaded.
You've been faithful even though there's been no contact.
This I recognize as letting me do the leading.

Home is important to you, and this you will find.
Work will be constructive, and you need both.
Too much of either will dull you and be a bore,
so learn to follow my lead, and you'll conquer both.

Kindness must prevail in dealing with the youth.
You'll only gain ground if you let me lead.
See to a calm and quiet home,
turn to me when you need to sow a seed.

Yes, you understand much, you need to do.
And patience is needed to be sure.
The poems will be guidance for you for a while.
Read them over and find what is pure.

Never feel that you haven't been true.
I know you get tired and need to rest.
I'll always call when it's important for you
and never feel you haven't passed the test.

Go about your day with reverence in your heart.
You've been quite close even though nothing's happened.
You'll be all right just trust in me from the start.
I'll give reassurance unto you. Just look back at what's happened."

Read Your Bible

"Oh, child, how I long to hear your praise. Praise is the essence of the Christian life. You only have to praise to receive my holy power. It will fill your being, and then you must claim it as part of your Christian life. Forgive and be forgiven, love and be loved, claim and it is yours. Before the need is ever recognized, I have given to you. All is well with your heart, mind, and soul, so please give of yourself to my service. I'll not ask more than you can give. Fear nothing as long as you have my presence within. There is only joy ahead for you. Now I'm talking about spiritual joy. You must never think you will escape the trials and troubles of the world. But that is only a passing thing.

Worldly pain will pass and spiritual joy and love can be yours forever. Claim it as a part of you. You must never return to the past of seeking only one aspect of the Trinity. We are one and must be worshiped as such. Please see to your Bible study and learn of me more completely. I am spread out, and my life is in sections in my book, but you must learn to put together all parts and worship me as a whole being not only love or discipline or judgement but in my entirety. Only then will you come to know me as your friend and really understand me.

Call to me often and worship and praise. Read of me daily. Learn, learn, and share this and many other words I have given you. Others need these words of wisdom also."

Discerning God's Will

Grant to me, Father, this day
the ability to come to you and pray.

For sick and hungry, I need to know
just how it is to pray for their woe.

It isn't pleasant to fast as they do.
It is necessary to understand what they go through.

So, Father, if I'm to fast this Ash Wednesday,
then help me, Lord, to discern thy will for the day.

Words from Jesus

"Many a time I have longed to tell you this,
a heavenly longing deep within;
oh, how happy I have been to know you
and how much happier to know you've invited me in.

Christmas means a lot to you,
for I bring a message straight from God to you.
Please listen and hear this simple song
and praise the Father for what you've been through.

Cling to the vine, and you shall grow.
Thank God for the trimming he's done.
Bless those around you and love them all.
Practicing Christianity can be fun.

Close to you I've moved,
even though you felt me not.
Your faith has seen you through,
and you'll hear from me a lot.

It's been quiet between us, I know.
I've purposely seen this was so.
This had its purpose as now you know,
and now we've stepped up but still have a long way to go."

God Cares

O Lord God, what can it be?
Won't you please say something to me?

Is this one of those times when my faith must be strong?
Yes, I guess so, but I know I still belong.

"Don't be so sure I'll not speak to you.
You had to clear your thoughts before I could get through.

Believe me when I say I care.
There is much I want to share.

Just think what you've learned so far.
You've learned much more where you are.

I've pulled you away from the group.
And you know that you're still learning without the group.

Keep it up, don't falter and slip.
I'll keep you going but ask and prepare for the trip.

So many times you become weary of the pace.
Just lean on me. I'll be there in your case.

You only have to call to feel my presence there.
For you see, I really do care."

Not by Bread Alone

"I've pulled you from the group for many reasons. Remember how Jesus must have felt as he too was alone in the wilderness. But remember what he said? "Man does not live by bread alone." He too was apart from his friends with no one to share with, yet look how he came through it. Stronger and closer for the agony he must have felt. Yet he lost faith not once. All the time he was tormented by Satan, he held on to his faith. I have not asked you to fast forty days and nights. I have not asked you to go into the wilderness. I won't do that. But identify with your Lord inasmuch as you have felt a deep separation, and all the time I have remained apart from you, I have also been with you. You have learned very much. Think of the thoughts and truths you have pulled from your Bible. Keep up the faith and remember to call on me for strength. You do become very weary when there is so much silence between us or nothing to excite you is happening. Read your Bible every day. Set aside the time even if the house must suffer. You will soon be hearing from your friends, and I will have your uplifting, so hang in there. Don't lose any faith. You know deep in your heart that I am with you always. This separation will not last."

Discernment

"There are times, my child, when you don't need to be told. Times when you know beyond a doubt that your answer is my answer, and you have it right away. This does happen, and it is best also to question for these feelings of assurance can be duplicated. It's best you ask for my answer. It is as you had planned this time, but perhaps again it might be that you will be fooled, so do come to me and ask for your answer. Many times I have asked you to do, and you have been so unsure of whether it is I or the evil one. Best you pray before any action is taken or you may never know which path you followed. This could cause confusion. I will always have patience and give you time to discern. You are right, it would be best if you have someone pray with you for discernment. You are new at this, and everyone needs help at first. You might ask me to close doors if you are traveling the wrong road. This too is a way to be sure of the right path. Recognizing my will is difficult until it has been well practiced. You will eventually be able to perform this without hesitation. Right now, it's difficult because I have been so hard to hear and feel. But I am here as you know, so just reach out. Your answer will be there. All you must do is recognize it."

Christian Friends

"Oh, my child, hold dear your friends. There is always a time when help is needed, and when that time comes, you will know you need to call on them. They will be there, ready to help. But you are right, it could be imposing to ask what you're thinking. It could be a time for witness too, and if any of the group has a chance to witness for me, I'm sure they would rejoice for the chance. You would not be free to say the things a stranger could say, for they could only remember what you used to be. But they also see a new person in you. They see the fruits of what you have tried to do. But on their level, your phony good deeds looked more promising to them. This is why I say people can easily be fooled and being honest and open doesn't always reap a harvest for the Lord. So it's best to wait on the Lord. He'll back you in your effort, and through the program, you'll have your help."

People

"People are so intricate. Their minds are full and working at all times, from the time of birth to the last breath. I love them all, whether they have accepted me or not. They're all my children, each and every one. From the least and lowest to the highest and best, each I love equally. Every time I see one of my children sinning, I suffer, and when they hurt, I hurt. Oh, for the longing I feel. Praising my Father that I could bear your sin as my own and carry your load for you. Praise your heavenly Father for his gift, making all things possible for those who choose the Lord Jesus as their Savior. Praise your Abba for friends and family. Praise him for sharing. Praise him for each heartache and hurt. Praise him for all blessings, large or small."

Strength from Above

"You'll have your help, it will come;
don't worry where it will come from.

You need not know the help you'll have;
there will be someone to help you plan.

Give up the worry, don't fret or care;
when the time comes, the help will be there.

Tomorrow you'll see the time will go well;
there will be time for everything, so relax a spell.

Have faith and believe in me;
I'll be your help, the Trinity.

You knew it before this poem,
but I wanted to see if you'd come for this poem.

You didn't know what you were up for,
but here you are, pounding on another door.

This time you came as I asked you to;
someday you'll discern everything I ask of you.

This is a good start, and I want you to know
the prayer and praise was what made it so.

That quiet time is important to you;
you must have it to see you through.

Keep up the good work and prayers also, you'll do all right;
just remember to rely on your Lord, Jesus Christ."

Listening

I know not what to pray;
why don't I just listen to what you have to say?

Oh, heavenly Father, speak to me;
tell me what you want of me.

"If only I could get you to listen.
You would surely with joy glisten.

Can't you hear, I'm calling you?
Through many friends, I speak to you.

Hear them out and then listen to me.
I'll tell you what I expect of thee.

You jump too fast to say yes or no.
You don't wait and let me tell you so.

Keep one ear open to your friend
and one turned to me. My answer I'll lend.

You miss out so many times.
This is why I'm so distant at times.

If only you could discern all the time.
You must learn to do this, you must find time.

Ask Gerry to pray, you know that you can.
It isn't easy, but you must take a stand.

Clear off the fog that separates us.
Be of good cheer, it isn't much fuss."

Stay Close to the Lord

No greater gift hath man than the Son of God within
to seal the love and turn the tide that leads that man to sin.

His great and glorious acts of mercy will help us all if we ask;
ask to have his loving Spirit instilled and take us to task.

This way, we know we will live forever with Jesus in eternity,
being able to listen and praise the Three in One, the Trinity.

Help is what we need right now to see us through this world;
he'll give you that help if only you don't become unfurled.

Stay calm and wait on the Lord; he needs your faith and trust.
You need him also, and don't forget, without him, you fall
back into sin, so life with him is a must.

Be careful now just what you say, don't drive the Spirit away;
be sure you love enough to always let him have his way.

You will be happier, this I can tell you,
for I've tried it, and life with Christ is wonderful, it's true.

Cares

Cares are important. How much we care and about who or what we care. These tell us much about a person. If we could read their real cares, we would know what kind of person we were dealing with.

People hide their cares as protection against the truth of what they really are. It's difficult in this world to open up ourselves and be honest about our cares, which are most important that is.

With the Father within us, we can do this. We can open ourselves up to the world, for we are protected by him, and only when we do this can people see his light shining through us. Then it is possible to bring many to their knees to ask for Jesus to be their savior.

Why do we as a people of God still protect ourselves, our egos, or our pride? Don't we realize this one thing is what keeps the Holy Spirit from entering in and bestowing on behalf of God, a glorious blessing, a gift, or whatever the Lord might have in store for us? You see, we miss so many times our calling because we can't put down ourselves and let Jesus take his place in our lives. We are hurting ourselves. For there is nothing more fulfilling than having Jesus within every moment of the day and night.

The Way to Thy Door

The way to thy door is not very far;
one touch of the Lord determines where you are.

It gives you a chance to return to your Lord
what's rightfully his, your soul so adored.

His claim to your life is what you must recognize;
once his, he'll love you, you'll not be chastised.

His door open wide, he'll invite you in.
Then open your door and let him come in.

There, once together, you'll see the beauty of it all;
once he's within, he'll always be on call.

Ready to heal any brokenness and shame;
ready to cleanse, to patch up the lame.

All you need to do is give your all to him,
open up your door, and let him come in.

Once he's inside, he'll fill you with joy;
he'll teach you, direct you, his Spirit he'll employ.

You'll be filled with a love you've never known before,
a love you'll appreciate and come to adore.

His special love is a new experience indeed;
once full of his love, you'll be able to plant a seed.

A seed of his love, his teaching, his grace,
for everyone will see it beaming from your face.

The way to his door is not very far, you see;
just open yours, he'll be there to greet thee.

The Key
Ephesians 6

"The answers do not come easy,
but look to me to find them;
I won't let you down about this,
I love Christina too much. We'll find them.

Your Bible is your daily guide,
to recognize this is good;
to know where to look can be difficult,
if you don't know my Word as you should.

Always call on me as you did;
I want to help in all things.
If only you could understand my need,
you would come more often. Oh, what joy it brings.

Your problem isn't simple,
but not too important to her, I hope.
It's not what she needs, this popularity.
She needs to be closer to me and rely on my strength to cope.

You could use Ephesians 6 to help.
It might be just the right time,
but only if you feel my guidance.
Let me pick the proper time.

It will come up, and you will need to be in tune,
so remember to think upward when it's time.
She'll mention it again, you wait and see.
Then you'll know what to say in time.

Wait on the Lord to arrange the scene.
This is always the way to begin.
Wait patiently on the Lord.
Don't jump in too soon and then find yourself in sin."

The King's Call

The King is your salvation, of this be sure.
You'll not deny his glorious right to serve.
If only you could see your future planned,
you would not doubt the Savior is close at hand.

It's only for a short time, this test of his.
You're impatient to begin to doubt this soon.
He'll call to you, and you'll feel his touch.
Don't rely on touch too much.

If only you could see the need right now,
for faith alone must be the plow.
Rely on faith, and doubt can't creep in.
Doubt can lead you back to sin.

If only your faith were as strong as your desire,
you would be a child on fire;
someday soon, he'll call your name,
he'll need you for a special plan.

Don't fret, you'll not be pulled away.
Your family will not have to stay.
Reason it out, be sure of your Lord;
he will give what he said he would.

Some suffering they all must do,
but don't you cry or be blue;
for they will find Christ through all that's to come,
and you will be there to help them some.

Suffering for Christ is not to be a burden.
The eyes must rest on him, and you'll not feel that burden.
Turn to God in praise when you feel the need.
Christ died for this; he really did bleed.

Messages

Oh, Lord Jesus, come be my guest;
can there be a message? Will someone be blessed?

"Oh, there are many messages I have to give.
But only in time so as not to misgive.

There's a time for each message and blessing to be sure.
Only at the proper time will it be worthy and pure.

You couldn't understand at all if I were to give all at once,
so it wouldn't be wise for you to ask for it all at once.

Many a time you're not completely ready for what I give.
But you have others to help you sort through and sieve.

They can help you as you already know.
They have been through where you yet have to go.

To explain it beforehand would only confuse.
So just relax and learn at your own pace my message to use.

Keep your eyes high, and don't look back to your sin.
It's all been washed away. Don't take it back in.

Sometimes you feel guilty about situations in your home.
Remember to keep your eyes on me where your help comes from.

These things will happen, and it's too hard to explain.
Don't try to preach it, live it, then you'll not be to blame.

Thanks is an important part of your daily life at home.
Incorporate your time so as to give the children time alone.

Remember to keep the eyes above at all times.
Hope for a better tomorrow, we'll pull out of the grind."

He Died For Me

The beauty of the cross transforms our lives
much more than we realize.

This beauty can build upon a rock
a home for us, a place for good stock.

This cross is a symbol for each of us,
a symbol of love, of unending trust.

Our faith must stand on solid ground;
where better to find it but at Calvary's mound.

At Calvary, where Jesus died for you,
a love he has, a love that's true.

For many a time, he sorrowed for you and me,
a deep sorrow we could not know, only he.

Lord Jesus is surely our King,
and I praise him, in song I sing.

Sing of his gift he gave to me;
oh, Jesus, my Jesus, how I love thee.

Keeping only unto him is what he wants;
oh, Jesus, I need help to tear down the fronts.

These fronts of social and financial must be taken away,
for your help I must continually pray.

There will be time to transform for me, thank God,
for I've loved you, Lord, and will till I return to the sod.

So thank you, Lord Jesus, for dying for me.
I praise you and thank you, for I love thee.

Ninety and Nine
Matthew 18

"Ninety and nine times a day,
swept through the air, they want to play.
But they're not here long enough to play.
They're really not here to stay.

Easy as it might seem to you,
it takes a lot to see this through.
You're not going to always be blue.
There are times when you'll see what's true.

Even Jesus was pushed away,
away from his God but not to stay.
It didn't take long to show you the way,
but it's hard to stay on the path and not stray.

There will be times when you need to be alone.
Many a time you'll be tired to the bone.
Just a good rest could be why you're alone.
Don't always think you've been wrong. My heart's not of stone.

I always want what's best for you.
I'll give you what you need to see you through.
The doors are not closed. I'm still with you
ninety and nine times, plus a few.

Count on me to be your friend.
Our relationship cannot end.
Now that I have you, I'll not let you go,
so don't feel apart. Don't worry so."

God's Message

"At Christmastime, you felt my love.
We even spoke of the heavenly dove.

During holy week, you wept tears for me.
It hurt you to think of me dying for thee.

If you can feel this compassion for me,
wouldn't you say, "Surely, I love thee"?

It sometimes is a quietness within,
not always leaping, don't feel that is sin.

A quiet tear I also see.
I truly know how much you love me.

Yes, you're right. There is not enough love,
but humans just can't feel or know the love from above.

It's too great, too much to comprehend,
but you have love and more I'll send.

But you must give it to receive more from above.
Keep pouring it out, I will refill you with my kind of love.

Many a time when you've doubted you could love,
you must accept that you can and practice that love.

Keep holding on to your heavenly rope.
Keep working and tugging, don't give up hope.

Someday you'll see the blocks you have made.
Then you can tear them down and the barrier will fade."

Thank you, Lord Jesus, for this message of yours.
I need reassurance from you to be sure.

Shun Disbelief

"There isn't room for any disbelief;
I want to give you full relief.

But there is a barrier in the way,
a deep and binding mistake I must say.

You must give it up to be truly free.
The house is a constant hang up to thee.

Repent and return to the joy of your youth.
You spoke of it as a glad time, a time of reproof.

Never ask to be shown the way
then say no to your Lord that day.

You have a desire that is of this world,
and you must give it up to be unfurled.

How many times must this lesson be learned?
How many times must we return?

Return to this spot in your growth with the Lord.
Return and again relearn; materialism must not be stored.

You're not worshiping me when you want all the time;
give up everything that is making you blind.

Then you can see the beauty of me;
you can have joy and truly be free.

Think of the joy you first knew;
the peace inside, it's surely dear to you.

Find it, you can, in following me;
give me the lead once again, I love thee."

Repentance

Forgive me, Lord Jesus, forgive me my sin;
cleanse me, Lord Jesus, cleanse me within.

Take it all from me, the wrong that I've done;
fill me, Lord Jesus, make us as one.

Let me serve you once again from the heart,
serving my Master, his love to impart.

Keep me in focus and bring me to bear;
show me my errors so I might leave them there.

At the foot of the cross, at the feet of my Lord,
for him to dispose of, so we're again of one accord.

Hold dear to my heart your whispers to hear
so I can say "Yes, Lord" and serve with great cheer.

Only you, dear Lord, can lead me to thee,
holding close to my heart your love of me.

Kiss the dove and send it to me;
let me hear words, and peace let me see.

Oh, Lord Jesus, how I will praise,
oh, heavenly Jesus, the rest of my days.

Fallen Away

"There is much you must learn,
and I'll help you to grow;
you must return to me,
before I can sow.

Believe me when I say I've not left.
You have taken a detour from me;
find your way back as soon as you can,
then it will be easier for you to see.

Cleanse you I have,
but you keep falling again.
There is not much I can do,
if you keep following sin.

I'll help what I can,
I'll keep you aware.
There will be a void,
you can see and compare.

If only you would work harder,
this contact with others might help;
you must seek your place
and stay there just in case I come for your help.

I can't use you right now,
for you fell from your path,
but struggle till your back on.
Keep calling to me to wash your sin in a bath."

Keep Searching

"Many, many times during the day,
as the children are at play,
then there will be time to say,
what's on your mind that day.

Believe me when I say
you will find time every day;
you gave yourself to me one day,
and I am in your heart to stay.

Never would I leave you now.
It doesn't seem possible I could leave you now.
It's you and I behind the plow;
to ever plunge ahead should be our vow.

Kiss the memory of your mind.
Draw it out a message to find.
A wealth of knowledge is planted there.
An answer to questions you're asking is there.

Keep searching for that particular peace you want.
It will come when your error you confront.
It will always be a source of pleasure to you,
and I will see you make it through.

Your problem will be found on your own.
Others will, of course, help over the phone.
You can't possibly hold up by yourself.
You'll need to call friends to hear their wealth.

This will bolster your spirits for a while.
Then you can reason out what's on file.
You have the knowledge stored away.
To bring it out, you must continually pray.

Even if I don't touch you with warmth,
you'll believe I am there without warmth.
As you do now, you know I'm here,
or you wouldn't be writing. There seems to be fear.

That's why I gave to you the scripture I did.
It's wrong to fear, of this you must be rid.
Keep calling to me. I'll come when you call.
You always find me holding on so you don't fall.

Keep passing it up, the problems to bear.
This will ease the burden you must bear.
You must always be willing to share.
This too is a help, it always will clear the air.

Keep this in mind as you start a new day,
and don't forget to start praising when you pray.
It's not phony as you sometimes feel.
Believe me, your way of life is quite real."

About the Author

The author's life has always been very common, small-town experiences. Raised by Christian parents found her in church and Sunday school at an early age, earlier than remembered. A singer in choirs, quartets, and even barbershop choruses. Life was good until she felt a void and something missing. Never found that missing part until her early thirties, when God moved in and made his Word come alive. From then on, God inspired, corrected, and advised in his special way. In his time, he has urged this writer to share her messages and even provided the means to accomplish this work. To God be the glory.

CPSIA information can be obtained
at www.ICGtesting.com
Printed in the USA
FFOW03n0919240218
45184635-45727FF